ARGENTINE CAUDILLO

ARGENTINE CAUDILLO

JUAN MANUEL DE ROSAS

JOHN LYNCH

A Scholarly Resources Inc. Imprint
Wilmington, Delaware

Originally published as *Argentine Dictator: Juan Manuel de Rosas, 1829–1852.*
© 1981 by Oxford University Press

© 2001 by Scholarly Resources Inc.
All rights reserved
Printed and bound in the United States of America

Scholarly Resources Inc.
104 Greenhill Avenue
Wilmington, DE 19805-1897
www.scholarly.com

Library of Congress Cataloging-in-Publication Data
Lynch, John, 1927–
    Argentine caudillo : Juan Manuel de Rosas / John Lynch.
        p. cm.—(Latin American silhouettes)
    Rev. and abridged ed. of: Argentine dictator. 1981.
    Includes bibliographical references and index.
    ISBN 0-8420-2897-8 (alk. paper)—ISBN 0-8420-2898-6 (paper : alk. paper)
    1. Rosas, Juan Manuel Josá Domingo Ortiz de, 1793–1877. 2.
Argentina—History—1817–1860. 3. Caudillos—Argentina—Biography. 4. Heads of
state—Argentina—Biography. I. Lynch, John, 1927– Argentine dictator. II. Title. III.
Series.

F2846.3.R7 L93 2001
982'.04'092—dc21
[B]

                                                                                00-052639

ABOUT THE AUTHOR

John Lynch is emeritus professor of Latin American history at the University of London, where he has spent most of his academic career, first at University College and then from 1974 to 1987 as director of the Institute of Latin American Studies. The main focus of his work has been Latin America in the period 1750–1850, and his books include *Bourbon Spain; The Spanish American Revolutions 1808–1826; Caudillos in Spanish America 1800–1850;* and *Massacre in the Pampas, 1872: Britain and Argentina in the Age of Migration.*

CONTENTS

PREFACE

The present book is a new edition of *Argentine Dictator: Juan Manuel de Rosas 1829–1852* (Oxford University Press, 1981). The English version, though not the Spanish, has been out of print for some years, and I am grateful to Richard Hopper and his colleagues at Scholarly Resources for encouraging the publication of an abridged version that, while preserving the identity of the first edition, would widen its appeal.

Scholars and specialists are familiar with the world of Rosas because it reveals the growth of great estates, the expansion of frontiers, the role of patron and client, the roots of dictatorship, and the use of state terrorism. Argentines have long been fascinated and outraged by Rosas, and the Spanish edition competes in their bookshops with numerous national histories of the caudillo. In the English-speaking world, Rosas is largely forgotten, though Britain supported him, fought him, traded with him, and finally rescued him. The world of Rosas and the pampas, however, was kept alive in English letters by a number of distinguished writers. Charles Darwin, who met him on campaign against the Indians in the southern pampas, described him as "a man of extraordinary character," the lord of vast estates, leader of the gauchos and country people, and for twenty years absolute ruler of Buenos Aires and its province.* Subsequently, Cunninghame Graham, W. H. Hudson, and John Masefield preserved in prose and poetry the history, the

---

*Charles Darwin, *Journal of Researches into the Natural History and Geology of the Countries Visited During the Voyage of H.M.S. "Beagle" Round the World,* 9th ed. (London, 1890), 52.

scenes, and the culture of that strange world. The present work is a distant follower of these pioneers and seeks to fill a void in the modern historiography.

This edition is an abridged version of the original and brings the background history up to date. In the process, I have omitted the introductory material, foreign relations, and most of the chapter on Rosas's exile in England, picturesque though it is. Footnotes are confined to citations for quotations, and the bibliography is shorter and more precisely focused. The book adjusts to some extent to recent trends in the study of the Rosas period concerning the *estancia* and agrarian regime, the political ideology of Rosas, the family, and community bases of power. But in general, I have preferred to leave the new research in the hands of its authors, identified in the bibliography, and to keep my own text intact as part of an ongoing debate on a controversial figure.

ACKNOWLEDGMENTS

I am very grateful to Joseph Smith and Peter Blanchard for their expert research assistance in the preparation of this book and to Malcolm Hoodless and Andrew Barnard for their help in its later stages. In Buenos Aires, Ezequiel Gallo helped me, and Dora Gándara provided valuable research services in the Archivo General de la Nación.

The Palmerston Papers are used and quoted by permission of the trustees of the Broadlands Archives. I am pleased to record my obligations to the Public Record Office, London; the British Library; the Royal Commission on Historical Manuscripts; and above all the Library of University College London; the Institute of Historical Research; and the Institute of Latin American Studies.

Research in the Ibero-Amerikanisches Institut, Berlin, was aided by a grant from the Central Research Fund of the University of London.

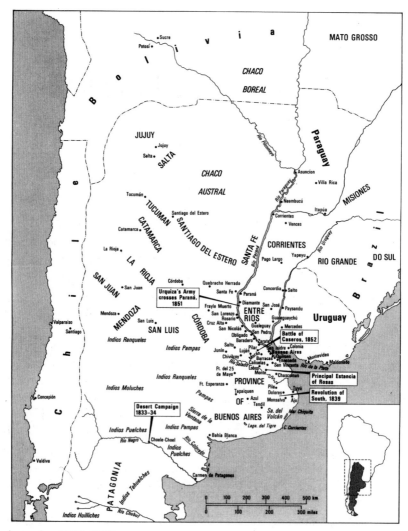

Argentina 1829–1852
Source: Copyright John Lynch.

1

LORD OF THE PLAINS

Born to the Estancia

Juan Manuel de Rosas, landowner, rural caudillo, and governor of Buenos Aires between 1829 and 1852, was born to property and privilege in a new land and an old society. The family and the frontier were the first influences that formed him. His heritage was colonial, and his people had been established in the Río de la Plata for some generations, patricians by virtue not only of their lineage but also of their offices and properties.[1]

His maternal grandfather, Clemente López de Osornio, a Buenos Aires militia officer and landowner, was a tough warrior of the Indian frontier who died weapons in hand defending his southern estate in 1783. On his father's side, Rosas was descended from a line of colonial military and official personnel. His paternal grandfather, Domingo Ortiz de Rozas, emigrated to America from the Spanish province of Burgos in 1742, and after an undistinguished career as a professional soldier, retired with the rank of captain. His son, Rosas's father, León Ortiz de Rozas, was born in Buenos Aires in 1760, and he, too, followed the family tradition, joining a Buenos Aires infantry regiment and reaching the rank of captain in 1801. He spent five months as a prisoner of the Indians before being ransomed back to civilization, living out his days as a gentleman *estanciero*.

The most powerful influence on Rosas, however, was his mother. Doña Agustina López de Osornio inherited her father's rich estancia, El Rincón de López, and also his imperious ways. Ten children survived of the twenty to whom she gave birth, and she ruled them harshly, whipping the boys into submission even when they were adolescents. She was the true head of the family, managing house

1

and estate with a fierce possessiveness. It was through his mother that Rosas was related to the Anchorenas, one of the richest families in the whole of the Río de la Plata; Juan José, Tomás Manuel, and Nicolás de Anchorena, sons of a Basque immigrant merchant, were his second cousins, soon to be his partners and allies.

The future caudillo, therefore, began life with excellent assets. The land was his legacy, his patrimony the pampas. He was born on March 30, 1793, in his family's town house in Buenos Aires, the first son of his parents. His education, though rudimentary, was appropriate for his role. He was taught to read and write at home and, at the age of eight, was sent briefly to a private school in Buenos Aires. But Rosas spent more of his youth on the estancia than in school, learning the ways of the plains and the life and language of the Indians. His nephew and biographer, Lucio V. Mansilla, asserted that the young Rosas was always destined to be a *hacendado* because that was the occupation of the elite: "As his parents were wealthy, and hacendados besides, in as much as this implies having an estancia in the Río de la Plata, they could not think of putting him into the church, or the militia, or the law, or medicine, professions which were merely the refuge of those who did not enjoy a good patrimony."[2] No doubt there were poor landowners outside the elite, but the Rosas family was not among them. He grew up to scorn a purely merchant career for young men. As he later explained, "I am convinced that the best career for them is an agricultural and pastoral one," and he trained his own sons in farming and established them in estancias of their own.[3] His formal education was supplemented by his own efforts in the years that followed. Rosas was not entirely unread, though the time, the place, and his own bias limited the choice of authors. He appears to have had a sympathetic, if superficial, acquaintance with the minor political thinkers of French absolutism.

The political events of the time, momentous for Argentina, were marginal to the world of Rosas. When a British expedition invaded the Río de la Plata in 1806, Rosas was thirteen, and along with many others of his age, he served as an ammunition boy in the popular army that Santiago Liniers organized and that defeated the British in August of that year. In 1807 during the second British invasion, Rosas served in the Caballería de los Migueletes, but he was probably absent from the campaign itself because of illness. He then went with his parents to work on their estancia in the country. Three years later in 1810, he was one of the many who stayed at home during the May Revolution, which inaugurated Argentina's independence from Spain. The execution of Santiago Liniers, ex-viceroy, royalist, and man of the counterrevolution, outraged him, and without challenging the fact of independence, Rosas did not disguise his preference for the colonial social order and its guarantee of peace and unity. Rosas, like many of his kind, looked back on the colonial period as a golden age when law ruled and prosperity prevailed. He had, moreover, a profound belief in Hispanic values. Forty years after the May Revolution these traits were still conspicuous and were recognized by a British observer: "General Rosas, however he may sometimes endeavour to disguise the fact, I am certain never sympathized in the struggle for Independence. He took at the time no part in the movement, and I believe was no patriot at heart. His ideas are now all Spanish."[4]

The May Revolution, therefore, played little part in the formation of the caudillo. From 1811, he concentrated on the administration of his parents' estates, taking no salary, only the opportunity to learn. He married in 1813, predictably against the wishes of his mother. His wife, Encarnación Ezcurra y Arguibel, belonged to an upper-class family of Buenos Aires and, like her husband, had been born to wealth and status. Shortly after his marriage, Rosas left his parents' estate and employment in order to work on his own account and fashion an independent career, first in the meat-salting industry, then in the accumulation of land. In the process, he became one of the precursors of a new stage in the development of Buenos Aires, the age of land boom, estancia expansion, and ranching export.

Conquest of the Pampas

The port of Buenos Aires and its hinterland were a unity. The city was not yet one of the great capitals of the Americas. The center of the city had a minimum charm inherited from its colonial past with its regular, paved streets crossing at right angles and its spacious plazas relieving the monotony; but the single-story houses were unimposing, and the skyline was enhanced by only a few towers and domes. The environment was insalubrious and there were few amenities. Fortunately, the transition from town to country was abrupt. About three miles from the center of the city, in outer districts of shabby buildings and pitted streets, the traveler crossed the Barracas bridge and entered the open plains. There, the country was well stocked with cattle and horses. People were less plentiful. The scattered dwellings of the rural settlers were no more than primitive ranchos, huts built of wood and adobe with thatched roofs and no beds. Refreshments were available at the *pulpería,* or country store, where riders could rest on the veranda and watch the gauchos, militia, peons, Indians, and other people of the pampas. A traditional goal of immigrants, the pulpería was no longer the primitive shack of the past or a simple retail outlet; it was becoming a means of social mobility, an essential trading link in the rural economy, and in some cases a source of credit and capital.[5]

Further south the traveler entered a paradise of natural parkland, the home of Indians, cattle, horses, ostriches, and myriad wild birds. In the vicinity of Lake Chascomús, the land was flat and treeless but endowed with a wild beauty. During spring the plains were covered with flowers, and the grass was a brilliant green; in winter, they were inundated by great floods; and in summer, when the tall grass wilted and crumbled, they were arid and dusty in the burning heat. Still further south, toward Tandil, soon to become a frontier fort and even in the 1840s no more than a primitive village, the frontier was being pushed out, and in the years after 1815 great estancias were in the process of formation; the land belonged mostly to the state, but its occupation was open to almost anyone with a pioneering spirit. The conquest of the pampas was about to begin.

The pampas were vast grasslands. W. H. Hudson recalled them vividly from his childhood: "a flat land, its horizon a perfect ring of misty blue colour where the crystal-blue dome of the sky rests on the level green world. . . . There were no fences, and no trees excepting those which had been planted at the old estancia houses."[6] There was nothing to see except the herds of cattle and horses, an occasional rider galloping over the plain, and even more rarely the house of an estancia in the distance like an island in a sea of grass and thistle. Temperatures were generally mild, though the summer months from December to February were very hot. There was much humidity, brought by the northerly winds. But from the southwest came the saving breeze of the pampas, the *pampero*, originating in the snow-covered Andes and often reaching hurricane force by the time it neared Buenos Aires. It was usually accompanied by an ugly dust storm, but it blew away the giant thistles and restored the pampas to the horsemen. Winter was not too severe but could be very wet, and mile after mile of the plains would be under water. Yet, in spite of the winter rains and the great rivers, the country suffered from periodic droughts, when the enormous flat expanse stretching from Patagonia to Salta, from the Atlantic to the Andes, absorbed the rivers, drying their channels. Normally, however, there was plenty of surface water available, and the soil of the pampas was rich and deep. Water was more plentiful toward the coastal plains than in the interior, and this moisture brought the cattle, and the Indians, closer to Buenos Aires.

The greatest enemy on the pampas was not the solitude or the climate but the Indians. Indians then controlled much of the territory that now forms the province of Buenos Aires. And even within the frontier there were large areas unoccupied by white men and unprotected by the state. By 1830, 5,516 square leagues were held in one form of property or another; two-thirds of what was to become the territory of the province thus had no legal occupants. The Indians were to be seen in the marketplace of Buenos Aires, trading their products for clothes, bread, meat, and the coveted wine. They were to be found, too, in their *tolderías*, or camps, huddled in their filthy tents and planning their next raid against well-stocked estancias.

The Indians of the plains comprised several tribes, Pehuenches, Ranqueles, Aucazes, Huilliches, and Puelches, displaying variations of a common culture, though not always that of the noble savage.[7] They were all hunters, inseparable from their horses, bowlegged from constant riding, traveling light and sleeping in tents, and preferring their traditional weapons, the lance and the bola, to the latest firearms. The ultimate source of Indian migration was Chile, from whose southern territories the Araucanians had been moving eastward over the Andes for many years, bringing with them their language, customs, and methods of contact, which varied among trade, bargaining, and war. The first decades of the nineteenth century saw one of the largest movements of Indians from Chile as numerous chieftains led their people eastward to Argentina to settle or raid either individually or in group alliances. This Araucanization of the pampas gave the Chilean Indians a vast reserve of land, cattle, and horses and posed for the frontier estancias, for the men and their womenfolk, an almost insuperable problem of security. The most hostile of all the Indians and those nearest to Buenos Aires were the Pampas, irremediably savage, treacherous, and venal—cruel to their own women as well as to any whites they captured. Whites had to parley very hard to secure the return of captive females, who, according to the laws of the Pampas, were the spoils of war and the sole property of the individual captors.

The expansion of the estancia economy from 1815 was a catastrophe for the pampa Indians. Settlers began to occupy the lands to the south of the Río Salado, and collision was inevitable. The Indians naturally resented the spread of settlements on lands they had always regarded as their own and on whose occupation they were not consulted. The more peaceable tribes retired to the mountains in the south, but the Ranqueles, the Pampas, and other migratory hordes retaliated by intensifying their raids against the intruders. In these plundering expeditions, they were often joined by vagabond gauchos, deserters from the army, delinquents fleeing from justices of the peace, refugees from social or political conflicts; from these they learned the ways of the whites, the methods of the militia, and the use of firearms. Their ambition was fed when their alliance was invoked in the postindependence civil wars by one side or another. Thus, in these conflicts the aggression of the Indians was matched by the violence of the settlers. Rosas himself was one of the new pioneers of the pampas, although he did not like killing Indians.

Rosas anticipated the expansion of the livestock economy of the 1820s and helped to promote the transition of Buenos Aires from viceregal capital to export center. The economic structure of Buenos Aires as it emerged from the colonial period was dominated by commerce, not agriculture. The great merchants of Buenos Aires made their profits not by exporting the products of the country—indeed, the city's own rural hinterland was little developed—but by importing consumer goods for a market stretching from Buenos Aires to Potosí and Santiago and exchanging them for precious metals. At the time of independence cattle products accounted for only 20 percent of the total export trade of Buenos Aires; 80 percent was in silver. Until about 1815, therefore, land exploitation continued to be a secondary activity, and landholding was limited both in the number of titleholders and in the extent of their holdings.

This simple structure was altered by three developments. First, the British squeezed out the merchants of Buenos Aires. With their superior capital resources and contacts in Europe, the British took over the entrepreneurial function previously exercised by the Spaniards and forced the *porteños* to seek alternative investments. Unable to compete in a British-dominated commerce, the local elite sought outlets in another incipient growth point, the cattle industry. Second, Buenos Aires province now profited from the removal of competition from its rivals. In the years after 1813, Santa Fe, Entre Ríos, and Corrientes were devastated by their wars of secession; the other rich cattle zone, the Banda Oriental, was ruined by revolution, counterrevolution, and the Portuguese invasion of 1816. Porteños took advantage of the new opportunity and found a profitable investment in cattle ranching. Third, the trade of Buenos Aires with the interior had depended on the interior's ability to earn from the sale of its products, especially from its rural and artisan industries. But increasing British penetration provided impossible competition for these industries at a time when war and secession were also removing traditional markets in Chile and Upper Peru.

The conjunction of British competition, provincial devastation, and decline of the interior rendered the Buenos Aires economy incapable of sustaining the local elite. They therefore began to diversify their interests, to invest in land, cattle, and saladeros. Government played its part in 1822, when Manuel J. García, minister of finance, introduced the system of emphyteusis in Buenos Aires province; the system was established in other provinces by the Constituent Congress in 1826. This measure authorized public land to be rented out at fixed rates for twenty years. Thus, the government simultaneously put land to productive use and satisfied the needs of farmers and cattlemen. There was no limitation of the area that a landowner might acquire in emphyteusis, and the land commissions, which administered distribution, were dominated by estancieros. By the 1830s some 21 million acres of public land had been transferred to 500 individuals, many of whom were allowed to transfer rent into freehold.

Rosas was one of the pioneers of territorial expansion and estancia formation. He bought two estancias, Los Cerrillos and San Martín, in the Guardía del Monte on the Río Salado up against the

Indian frontier, and these became his most important properties.[8] From 1818, he amassed further land for himself and at the same time acted as adviser and buyer for his cousins, the Anchorenas. In 1820, he extended his holdings beyond the Salado and established a settlement with a farm that he called La Independencia; this holding was his outpost against the Indians. Rosas was now the leading expert on land values, investment opportunities, and estate management. He more than anyone appreciated the new economic and political power of the estancia, and it was under his guidance that the Anchorenas brought commercial and urban capital into land. He was not simply a representative of the new frontier. He and the Anchorenas were at its heart, owners of private fiefdoms in land among the best in the province. Arriving at night at Los Cerrillos, Charles Darwin was so impressed by its extent that he thought it was "a town and fortress."[9]

To manage such a domain was a constant challenge, and the line between order and anarchy was very thin. Rosas complained of "the mob of idlers, vagabonds and delinquents" who consumed cattle wastefully, and of rustlers who robbed by night. And he had no time for the small, struggling rancher: "The wealthy estancieros have slaves, peons, transport, places to cure the hides, to store the tallow, to make use of the offal. The others might work hard but they do not have the wealth or the power of these estancieros, unless they become their dependants." Rosas mastered rural life and brought a professional competence to estate management: "I am a hacendado and from my youth I have worked, applying reason and reflection to our principal sources of wealth." He organized his rural program down to the last detail and imposed his iron will on every subordinate. The key word in his vocabulary was *subordinación,* by which he meant respect for authority, for social order, for private property. His own estancia was a state in miniature; he created a society out of nothing, a disciplined workforce equipped to defend itself against Indians without and anarchy within. He came to dominate the nomadic gauchos, the idle peons, the rebellious Indians, the entire pampa environment, and he did so invoking a number of basic principles: conquest of the empty zone between the estancias and the tolderías; the formation of a regular militia; peaceful relations with the Indians through rewards and employment; a strong executive power in the rural sector with extraordinary powers delegated to the estancieros to deal with the routine tasks of law and order.[10]

Caudillo-in-Waiting

The frontier, however, was not the only sector exposed to invasion and disorder. In 1820, the year of anarchy, Rosas had to turn his cowboys into cavalry and divert the power of the estancia to the rescue of Buenos Aires. Independence from Spain had culminated not in national unity but in dismemberment. After a decade of conflict between Buenos Aires and the provinces, between central government and regional interests, between unitarists and federalists, the framework of political organization in the Río de la Plata collapsed. Independent republics proliferated all over the provinces, and when Buenos Aires tried to reduce them to submission, they fought back, their caudillos leading irregular gaucho hordes, the *montoneros,* against the capital. Buenos Aires looked to the south, and in September 1820, Rosas prepared his *peonaje.* His basic recruiting ground was his own estancia: "I spoke to the hands on the estancia where I live on the frontier of the Monte; they came forward to follow me, and with them and some cavalry militia I marched to the assistance of our honourable capital which was calling us to our duty with increasing insistence."[11] He led them forth, dressed in red and well mounted, from Los Cerrillos. These were the original Colorados del Monte, 500 men, and they joined the army of Buenos Aires as the Fifth Regiment of Militia.

This was Rosas's first direct action against the dreaded anarchy, the first display of that peculiar mixture of protection and menace that became a hallmark of his rule. Rosas fought not only the invaders without but also those he regarded as subversives within. According to some, the Colorados behaved in a disciplined way in the city streets, respecting property and preserving law and order. Others thought that the upper classes paid dearly for this intervention, for "the bloodthirsty gaucho Rosas" used more force than was necessary and "from that time he took pleasure in oppressing the enlightened classes with the men of the countryside." This disapproval was one of the earliest expressions of a theme recurrent in Argentine historiography, that Rosas used a gaucho power base to intimidate the upper classes and that he imposed rural barbarism on urban civilization. Whatever the truth, from this action Rosas acquired military power, a political reputation, and more land. Yet he quickly returned to his estancia and stayed there. He was not in sympathy with the government of Martín Rodríguez, which he had helped to save, much less with that of Bernardino Rivadavia, who was appointed president of the United Provinces of the Río de la Plata in February 1826 and came to power with a unitary constitution and a modernization program.

Rivadavia projected economic growth through free trade, foreign investment, immigration, and liberal institutions, the whole enclosed in a united Argentina, for the sake of which Buenos Aires would relinquish its monopoly of customs revenue and share it with the nation. The entire model was rejected as a dangerous irrelevancy by Rosas and his associates, who represented a more primitive economy—cattle production for export of hides and salt meat—but one that brought immediate returns, preserved the province's resources for the province itself, and remained true to the country's traditions. Rosas's mentality at this point was that of a provincial jefe, not a national leader. In the latter half of 1826, at the head of a network of friends, relations, and clients, Rosas allied himself to the federalist party, which he was eventually to absorb and destroy.[12] He joined this party not for reasons of political ideology, which he did not possess, but because unitary policy threatened to strip Buenos Aires of its assets and thwart its supremacy. The federalist politicians accepted his support without considering the risks involved, and the provincial caudillos were naive enough to believe that they had found a new champion against the pretensions of the capital. Rivadavia bowed to the combined forces of his opponents and resigned from the presidency. In a sense, Rivadavia was brought down by Rosas, even though Rosas did not yet rule. It was the real federalists who came to power; they were led by Manuel Dorrego, who in August 1827 was at last elected governor of Buenos Aires.

The new regime promptly recognized the services and the status of Rosas. On July 14 he was appointed commandant general of the rural militias in the province of Buenos Aires. To his strong economic base, he now added the greatest military power in the province. And he used his authority to reassure yet again the estancieros of the south by applying a coherent frontier policy consisting of new settlements grouped around forts, protection by military garrisons, and a buffer of friendly Indians. He also persuaded the ranchers to collaborate with his militia by providing supplies, for which they would be paid by the government and rewarded with peace and security. As militia commander, frontiersman, and rancher, Rosas now had unique qualifications to take power should the occasion arise. Security on the frontier and in the countryside depended on political stability at the top and on getting the right decisions from the politicians in Buenos Aires. According to the political thinking of Rosas and his associates, these circumstances could no longer be assumed: they had to be imposed. The opportunity soon came. In December 1828, Dorrego was overthrown by a coup engineered by General Juan Lavalle, leading the military recently returned from the war with Brazil, and by a small group of professional politicians allied to the mercantile and intellectual elite, the whole representing a unitarist reaction against caudillos, montoneros, and other manifestations of provincialism. The coup was a further stage in the conflict between the career politicians and the new economic forces, between the professional officials and militarists created by the struggle for independence and the landed interests. Dorrego was defeated by the unitarist army and shot on orders of Lavalle, leaving a gap in the federal leadership that was instantly filled by Rosas.

How Did Rosas Gain Power?

Rosas had no serious rival. As commander of the militia, he had secured a virtual monopoly of military power in the countryside. His peaceful negotiations on the frontier had gained him Indian friends, allies, and recruits. His achievements had also won him the respect of the estancieros, who basked in unwonted peace and security. And the crisis of subsistence in the pampas in 1828–1829 enabled him to recruit popular forces, above all in the south. A great drought dried up lakes, rivers, and wells; vegetation disappeared, and crops and cattle suffered. Adversity aroused anger, and the rural poor were ready to rise not in a coherent or coordinated movement but in a series of protests extending across the south and west of the province. Indians attacked white estancias for horses and cattle. Bands of montoneros under minor caudillos underwent classic transformation from outlaws to guerrillas to freedom fighters, or, as they were sometimes called, *anarquistas,* without ceasing to be bandits.

These were the elements encountered, exploited, and to some

extent assembled by Rosas in his successful bid for power in 1829, when he himself became a *jefe de montoneros* and fought a guerrilla war against the regular forces of General Lavalle and the unitarians. First he recruited among his landed supporters and expected client estancieros to come to his service with peons, horses, and cattle; those who held back realized later in 1829 that they had missed a winning venture and hastened to explain. He instructed his supporters to make their base in the south of the province, his home ground, and to wage economic war on Lavalle and his allies. This war was the *guerra de recursos,* designed to achieve its objectives by destroying the estancias of the unitarians. To wage this war, however, Rosas had to recruit rural hordes from the lower sectors, from Indians, gauchos, deserters, and delinquents. The ambiguity of the caudillo's position served his purpose. Was he the leader of rural rebels? Or was he the protector of society against their anarchy?

Events dictated the answers. In April 1829, when Lavalle marched on Santa Fe, revolts occurred throughout the province of Buenos Aires, and the whole countryside appeared to be under the military occupation of units acting in the name of Rosas. Rosas defeated Lavalle's regular army in that same month and from then onward gradually increased his stranglehold on the capital while simultaneously preventing a bloodbath. The caudillo entered Buenos Aires on the night of November 3, 1829, and was received not simply as a military servant of the government but as a victor and leader of the federalist party and a man who had credit among popular forces. He was now ready for power, but not just any power. On December 6, when he was elected governor at the age of thirty-five, he was granted *facultades extraordinarias;* this amounted to absolute power, as proposed by Tomás de Anchorena and supported by a virtually unanimous vote of the House of Representatives. He took power amid an orgy of pure personalism, basically alien to federalist thinking. Order and security, observed a newspaper report, were best ensured not by general laws but "by the character of our worthy governor; that is where we will find all the guarantees which good citizens can desire." [13]

How can we explain the rise of Rosas? In the first place, he represented the rise to power of a new economic interest and a new social group, the estancieros. The classic elite of the Revolution of

1810 were the merchants and the bureaucrats. The struggle for independence created professional politicians, state officials, a new military, men who can be described as "career revolutionaries."[14] By 1829 their day had passed. In effect, the Buenos Aires landowners overthrew the existing rulers and took direct possession of the government of the province through their representative, Rosas. In 1829, Rosas and his hordes succeeded in dismantling the remnants of the army of independence, already weakened by the war with Brazil; thus, the defeat of Lavalle was the defeat of a professional army, a rival force, by the militia of Rosas and his estanciero allies. Rural activities extended into the capital, where they were indistinguishable from the interests of exporters and importers; indeed, estates and warehouses were often in the same hands. British merchants and native entrepreneurs were firm supporters of Rosas and joined the coalition of groups behind the supreme leader.

Conditions, then, created Rosas. He was the individual synthesis of the society and economy of the countryside, and when the interests of this sector coincided with those of the urban federalists, Rosas was at once the representative and the executive of the alliance. In this sense, as Mansilla observed, "Rosas did not make himself; events created him, others made him, a number of extremely wealthy and self-interested people, bourgeois types with aristocratic pretensions—a kind of landed aristocracy though in no way comparable to the English gentry—behind him these would be ruling."[15] This is a simple explanation of the rise of Rosas, but not a complete one. It ignores his specific qualifications—his origins, career, and power over events. He was a caudillo before he was elected governor.

His personal career was unique and did not conform exactly to the model of merchant-turned-landowner, which characterized so many of his supporters. He began on the estancia, learned the business from the working end, accumulated capital in the rural sector itself, and advanced from there. He was a pioneer in the expansion of landowning and cattle raising, starting some years before the big push southward from 1820. Unlike the Anchorenas, for example, who relied on overseers or on Rosas himself, he was not an absentee landlord; he was a working estanciero, operating at every stage of cattle raising. Thus, he came into direct contact with the gauchos, delinquents, Indians, and other denizens of the pampas, partly to recruit them for his estancias, partly to mobilize them for his militia. He exerted authority not only over his own peons but also over the rural masses beyond his private boundaries. His support base was popular as well as patrician.

No doubt others shared this experience. But Rosas added another qualification. He was militia commander of the province. He had more military experience than any other estanciero. In the recruitment of troops, the training and control of militia, and the development of units not only on the frontier but also in urban operations, he had no equal. It was the military dimension of Rosas's early career that gave him the edge over his rivals. This experience culminated in his role during the guerrilla war of 1829, when he raised, controlled, and led the anarchic popular forces in the irregular army that defeated Lavalle's professionals. In this case his personal qualifications, if not unique, were certainly decisive. Rosas was not only a creature of events; he made them. He not only represented others; he led them. This dualism was apparent also when the fruits of victory were distributed.

Already before December 1829, Rosas had the qualities of a political leader. In the previous decade, he had established a powerful base in the countryside, partly on his own initiative, partly as a delegate of the government. He had served the state, and he had profited from the state. Although he represented the landowners, he also represented himself, the most powerful of all the landowners. It is doubtful whether they could have found anyone better qualified than Rosas. To this extent, he was not merely their creature, for he had a strong bargaining position. Rosas was a self-made caudillo. There was a political as well as an economic truth in his assertion, "I went out to work with no more capital than my own credit and industry."[16]

2

ESTANCIERO

Who was Rosas? A landowner
What did he accumulate? Land
What did he give to his supporters? Land
What did he take from his enemies? Land[1]

Absolute Power

Rosas took office in December 1829 with assets and liabilities finely balanced. He demanded absolute power and was given it with much political support. Absolutism did not conflict with his own principles. In an interview with the Uruguayan envoy Santiago Vázquez on the day after he took office, he denied he was a federalist: "I tell you I am not a federalist, and I have never belonged to that party. Had I belonged to it I would have given it leadership, a thing which it has never had. . . . All I want is to prevent disaster and restore institutions."[2] Rosas did not want to fail through lack of power. Conditions called for strong government. The economy was laid low by man and nature alike. The war with Brazil, followed closely by civil war between unitarians and federalists, damaged production and exports and crippled the treasury. Rosas inherited too much expenditure and too little revenue. During the whole of his first government, moreover, the province endured a great drought. From December 1828 to April 1832 there was no rain; crops suffered, cattle perished, horses died of hunger and thirst. When livestock declined, the whole country languished. Woodbine Parish, the British consul general, told Charles Darwin that the ground was so dry and so much dust was blown about that in the open country landmarks became obliterated and people could not tell the boundaries of their estates.[3]

Political problems were also pressing. Although Buenos Aires had an ally in Santa Fe, the forces of the unitary League of the North were still in the field under the command of General José María Paz, and it was not until his fortuitous capture in March 1831 that the civil war came to an end. Political and economic relations between Buenos Aires and the provinces still had to be resolved, and after prolonged dispute, Rosas was content to recognize the autonomy of the provinces in an informal federal pact. In Buenos Aires itself, Rosas created an impression of firm government and financial soundness, and he probably could have procured a further term of office had he been prepared to accept a constitution. As it was, the House of Representatives, where federalists were split between moderates and conservatives, accepted the return of the extraordinary powers, and on December 5, 1832, Rosas completed his first term of office. He was succeeded by Juan Ramón Balcarce, with whom the moderate influence came to the fore; but Balcarce was forced out in October 1833 by the revolution of the Restauradores, provoked by the *rosistas*. The legislature then appointed Juan José Viamonte provisional governor in an attempt to avoid further dictatorship, but the balance of power was not in his favor and he resigned on June 27, 1834. At first Rosas refused the offer of governorship, as did a number of other unwilling candidates. Eventually he accepted on condition that the legislature grant him the *suma del poder público*. This it did on March 7, 1835, and Rosas began his long period of rule virtually on his own terms.

These were also the terms of the dominant sector of society. Dictatorial powers were thought to be necessary to end social conflict, political instability, and economic deterioration and to ensure the hegemony of the estanciero interest. The first administration of Rosas had been a conservative one: it represented property, especially landed property, and it guaranteed tranquillity and stability. He strengthened the army, protected the church, silenced the critics, muzzled the press, ignored education, and sought to improve the financial credit of the government. In 1833–1834, when Rosas was out of power, political instability returned, exports dropped, and the financial situation worsened. Rosas came back to power on the record of his first government. He had already reassured the estancieros by his land and frontier policy and by his ability to impose order. His orthodox fiscal policy also appealed to them. One of his first measures when reelected was to liquidate the Banco Nacional (May 30, 1836). He thus ended any prospect of restoring the gold value of the peso and of deflating; instead his financial policy was based firmly on curtailment of expenditure and collection of taxes.

The landed elite responded positively to Rosas. They were his political base. The legislators that elected him to office in 1829 and 1835 were all products of the upper sectors in town and province. In July 1835 from all corners of the province the most prominent of the estancieros traveled to Buenos Aires to mount guard before the governor's house as a mark of respect and deference. Some estancieros, it is true, opposed Rosas, though they did not form an identifiable interest. There were some who had political objections to Rosas— unitarists who disliked federalism, federalists who abhorred dictatorship. In 1838, when Rosas's policy, inducing the French blockade, was thought to be damaging to the export business of the estancias and saladeros, there may even have been an element of economic interest in the opposition. From this thinking sprang the 1839 rebellion of the south, among whose leaders were a number of large landowners. But in general, criticism of Rosas was ideological rather than sectional. Indeed, there was no reason for class opposition to Rosas: as an estanciero himself he knew what was required.

The Desert Campaign

As governor of Buenos Aires, Rosas took a number of positive steps to improve the status and security of landholdings. He began from the obvious assumption that the economy of Buenos Aires depended on the pastoral industry and that it needed more land. The pressure on grazing land since the boom of the early 1820s and the shortage of further emphyteusis lands had brought the livestock sector to the limits of profitable expansion. Ranchers were pushing south into Indian territory in search of cheap land. This expansion called for government action to occupy new territory and protect it. Rosas stood for a policy of expansion and settlement, and in 1832 his government made large grants of frontier land to veterans of the wars against the unitarians and to ranchers hard hit by the recent drought. And in the following year the frontier resounded to a more militant initiative, the Desert Campaign against the Indians, led by Rosas himself. The far south was only a desert in that it lacked a settled population. It had three major rivers, the Salado, the Colorado, and the Negro, capable of transforming a region of 20,000 square leagues into fertile pasture-land extending southward to the northern confines of Patagonia.

This campaign seemed a departure for Rosas. Yet, as an estanciero and militia commander, he knew how to distinguish between enemy Indians, who had to be fought, and friendly Indians, who could be cultivated by trade and gifts and prevented from harboring delin-quents. He did not normally favor war against the Indians, preferring peace, parleys, and presents in order to attract them toward work and civilization. But he also had to recognize that a policy of pacification was not permanently valid, that the Pampas Indians were marauding too close to the estancias for comfort, and that Indian aggression demanded a military response. He probably had other motives too. If the legislature refused to renew his extraordinary powers and he had to leave the governorship at the end of his term of office, what would be his role and where would be his power? Command of a strong army would give him an unassailable base. And if he led this army in a successful expedition to expand and secure the frontier, he could not fail to strengthen his influence with the estancieros of his own province and with the caudillos elsewhere.

Rosas argued the urgency of frontier security before leaving office, and in November 1832, he presented to the assembly a spe-cific plan for an expedition against the Indians. His ideas were not merely defensive. There was a manifest expansionist spirit, as well as undue optimism, in his call to arms: "Hacendados! You know that the countryside and the frontier are now entirely free of enemy Indians; that, terrified by the repeated death blows they have suf-fered in their own homes and camps, they have fled to the other side of the Río Negro and to the foothills of the Andes. One effort more, and our wide plains will be free for ever, and we will secure the foun-dations of our national wealth."[4]

Appointed commander of operations against the enemy Indians, Rosas led his forces from his estancia, Los Cerrillos, on March 22, 1833, in a long convoy of 1,500 men, thirty wagons, 6,000 horses,

and thousands of cattle. At this point the expedition had already cost
the provincial treasury more than 300,000 pesos, soon to rise to 1
million pesos, raised by the government with the greatest difficulty.
Yet the undertaking was good business for Rosas and the estancieros,
who provisioned the expedition and were well paid. Rosas kept a
sharp eye on matters of supply, ensuring that the appropriate agen-
cies were under his control and that contracts were given to his
friends and clients. The returns on this great investment, he argued,
would benefit the whole people: "New avenues of commerce will be
opened and untold wealth will be released for intelligent use."[5]

The army advanced to the island of Choele Choel on the Río
Negro, clearing the intervening country, showing the flag, making
alliances with friendly Indians, and striking hard at enemy tribes.
Rosas established his headquarters on the Río Colorado, which was
surveyed westward to within sight of the Andes, and he sent General
Angel Pacheco to scout the length of the Río Negro. The young
Charles Darwin, who disembarked from the *Beagle* on the Río
Negro in August 1833, observed Rosas's army as it camped in a
square formed by wagons, artillery, straw huts, and equipment.
"The soldiers were nearly all cavalry," he noted, "and I should think
such a villainous, banditti-like army was never before collected
together. The greater number of men were of mixed breed, between
Negro, Indian, and Spaniard. I know not the reason, but men of
such origin seldom have a good expression of countenance."[6] He
was looking, in fact, at the classical gaucho types, the *vagos y mal
entretenidos,* the outlaws and other marginal inhabitants of the pampas who were herded into the armies of the time. Rosas imposed a
harsh discipline on this force, but amid military preoccupations, he
never lost sight of the basic economic justification of the expedition.
In his diary he extolled the Río Colorado, which brought water to
fine plains from the cordillera to the coast and was capable of supporting many sheep farms and even more estancias, resulting in
abundant exports of hides, salt meat, and tallow.

The expedition gave Rosas a new title, *conquistador del desierto,*
and paid him large political dividends for a return to power. The
title was not entirely inappropriate. In one year he had effectively
added to Buenos Aires an area extending 200 leagues west to the
Andes and south beyond the Río Negro, thousands of square miles
in all, and with new territory came new topographical information,

new resources, new security. As Rosas exclaimed in the final message to his troops: "The fine territories, which extend from the Andes to the coast and down to the Magellan Straits are now wide open for our children."[7]

After the Desert Campaign the Indians sought a peace treaty with Rosas. They pledged to keep to their own territory, not to cross the frontier or enter the province of Buenos Aires without permission. They also undertook to tender military service when called upon and to act as peaceful citizens. In return each cacique received at regular intervals a quantity of mares or colts according to the number of his followers and a small allowance of yerba, tobacco, and salt. The provisions of rewards and supplies to friendly Indians, about 10,000 in all, became a thriving rural business. Miserable little pulperías improved their prospects by this trade, and the friendly tribes provided an insatiable market for *aguardiente,* tobacco, biscuit, manioc, and maize, all necessary to keep them happy and quiet; and consumer goods, gifts to caciques from "brother Juan Manuel," meant profitable orders for the artisan workshops of Buenos Aires and for favored contractors who notoriously cheated the Indians. Pacification served the nation well in the next twenty years, but in the long term it enabled the Indians to strengthen their position. The whole transaction amounted to an Indian subsidy paid by the government of Buenos Aires. This liberality, or "profligate bribery," as the British minister called it, gave Rosas some control over the Indians and marginally extended his political base.[8] Friendly Indians were paraded at federal demonstrations to pronounce for Rosas, as at Tapalque in 1835, when cacique Cachuel declared: "Juan Manuel is my friend, he has never deceived me. I and all my Indians will die for him. . . . The words of Juan are the same as the words of God."[9] Toward "foreign" Indians, those outside the pacification treaty, the regime showed no mercy. In 1836 some eighty were captured in a raid on Bahía Blanca, brought in chains to Buenos Aires, and publicly shot in groups of ten in front of the Buen Retiro barracks.

Land and Its Owners

The Desert Campaign was followed by rapid expansion of the southern frontier, and by the 1840s, estancias encroached once more on Indian hunting grounds. But whereas the estancieros now received more respect from the Indians, they did not receive labor or service, as the Indians were loath to become working peons. The white population itself remained thin on the ground. "A few years ago," reported William MacCann, English merchant and traveler, "General Rosas seized all the women in Buenos Aires of doubtful character, and sent them towards this frontier, with strict orders for their detention; hoping to augment the population by that means."[10] If labor was scarce, land was abundant. Through rentals, sales, and grants, the provincial government transferred large tracts to private hands in the years following 1833. Emphyteusis had now outlived its usefulness both to the state and to the individual: it had facilitated land exploitation but also encouraged excessive land concentration without ensuring full payment of rent. Rosas preferred to sell public lands outright and to secure a revenue from their sale. A series of laws from 1836 placed on the market vast expanses of land at fairly low prices and greatly added to the grazing area. The big buyers were the same people as the large tenants under emphyteusis: the Anchorenas, Díaz Vélez, Félix de Alzaga, Felipe Arana, and Domingo Lastra. By 1840, 3,436 square leagues of the province were in the hands of 293 people. Yet such was the vastness of the frontier that the government found itself with unsold land on its hands and unpaid debt to its account. As an alternative to selling land, therefore, Rosas decided to give it away. This strategy was the ultimate logic of the buyers' market.

The regime operated by a system of rewards and punishments. Land grants were made as a reward for loyalty or in lieu of salaries to soldiers and bureaucrats. Land became almost a currency, or a wages and pensions fund. The Desert Campaign was the starting point, and Rosas himself the first beneficiary, followed by senior officers. The rebellion of the south in 1839 was followed by retribution for some and rewards for others; land was granted to members of the military who participated in crushing the rebellion and to civilians who remained loyal. Further federal victories were accompanied by generous awards to the victors. The land policy of Rosas thus culminated in a vast bounty scheme. He had begun by expanding the southern frontier and increasing the stock of land. He then liquidated emphyteusis rentals, proceeded to sell land cheaply, and ended by giving it away. He served the interests of the estancieros and *saladeristas.* "No other social group," it has been aptly observed, "derived greater benefits from the Rosas regime, nor was any other group more intimately interested in maintaining the regime intact."[11]

Land laws and land values favored the estancieros; the financial policy of Rosas was also partial to them. In 1829 and again in 1835, he inherited a huge deficit, a depreciated currency, and a large public debt. By liquidating the Banco Nacional, he abandoned any attempt to restore the gold value of the peso. He followed instead a conservative financial policy, cutting expenditures, improving revenue collection, and shunning any social reallocation of resources. The bulk of revenue, normally 80–90 percent, continued to come from customs duties. Apart from 1839 and 1846, when blockades disrupted foreign trade and decreased the customs revenue, it continued to grow: it rose from 10 million pesos in 1835 to 60 million in 1850.

The *contribución directa,* a tax on capital and property, had been introduced by the Rodríguez administration in 1822 as an alternative to excessive reliance on customs duties. But it failed to fulfill its promise. Rates were too low and made no provision for currency depreciation. As there had been no state census or valuation of property, estimates of property values were left to the taxpayers, who became virtually their own tax inspectors. Rosas attempted more than once to increase the rate of assessment, but this was one issue on which the assembly resisted. In 1850, when total revenues reached the peak figure of 62 million pesos (in depreciated currency), the contribución directa furnished only about 3 percent of the total. Well over half of this portion came from commerce and industry. Thus, the share contributed by landowners and cattle breeders to total taxation was small.

Rosas preferred almost any expedient to increasing taxation and disturbing his power base. There were a few simple alternatives. He could meet government deficits by paring down expenditures. He was particularly savage toward social expenditure such as education, welfare, and public works. In 1838 the government withdrew its subsidy from the University of Buenos Aires, which almost expired in the last years of the regime, its total staff three unpaid professors. Rosas could also raise loans and print money. Up to March 1840 the government made successive issues of bonds, and by the end of 1840 the long-term debt of the province amounted to about 36 million pesos. This debt was serviced promptly, and by 1850 only 13.7 million pesos of *fondos públicos* were still outstanding. Rosas had to avoid too much long-term borrowing, for the estancieros, who alone were capable of supporting it, disapproved; they preferred inflation. So the government resorted to the printing press. By successive issues, paper currency increased from 15.2 million pesos in 1836 to 125.2 million pesos at the end of the regime. Rosas was thus responsible for issuing 110 million pesos in just over eleven years. This strategy was the Rosas financial system, his way of financing deficits and avoiding bankruptcy, borrowing, and taxing. Issue of paper money, of course, pushed up prices and depressed wages, thus causing a redistribution of incomes against the poorer sectors. The landowners did not object; they accepted inflation as a preferable alternative to forced loans and higher taxes.

Encouraged by the law, by prices, and by fiscal policy, the estancieros took over the land that Rosas had promised them. He presided over a massive transfer of property from public to private domain. In place of tenants of the state, he created a landowning elite that now held some of the largest estates in the world. The land policy of Rosas had an obvious economic objective in that it sought to maximize the most accessible export commodities. It rested, too, upon particular social assumptions and reinforced the power of the landowner over the laborer. But it also had political implications. Land was the richest source of patronage available, a weapon for Rosas, a welfare system for his supporters. Rosas was the great patrón, and the estancieros were his *clientela*. In this sense *rosismo* was less an ideology than an interest group, a focus of property rather than of principles.

The counterpart of land grants was land confiscations. These were designed to punish and to prevent. Opponents could have been imprisoned or exiled without harming their families and impairing their prospects. But to be deprived of one's estate really hurt. This strategy was also economic warfare. Confiscations not only cut off the resources of the opposition and the means of recruiting peons; they also gave the government a source of revenue and patronage. Was there an element of populism in Rosas's policy? If there was, it was only a by-product of his main objective. Confiscations inevitably hit the haves rather than the have-nots, and they threatened ruin to every family that had a member on the unitarian side.

The basic law of expropriation was the decree of September 16, 1840, issued at a time when the regime was under extreme pressure from the combined power of the French and the unitarians. It made every kind of property of unitarians—goods, urban and rural real estate, stocks and shares—potential payment for the damage done by General Lavalle. The beneficiaries were the *rosista* state and its friends. Expropriation enabled the dictator to feed and mount his army, reward his followers, subsidize his friendly Indians, and keep his whole system going. Years later, in Southampton, Rosas was asked to comment on his reasons for this decree. He replied: "If I was able to govern that turbulent country for thirty years, taking charge when it was in full anarchy and leaving it in perfect order, it was because I always observed this rule of conduct: to protect my friends at all costs, and to destroy my enemies by any means."[12]

The unitarians also confiscated property, if anything more ruthlessly than the federalists. In 1828–1829 there were advisers around Lavalle who were just as prepared as Rosas to make the rivalry a war of property. If they had prevailed, Rosas himself would have been the first victim, for it was said by some unitarians that "it would be very useful to indemnify the landowners who have been plundered by the barbarians of Rosas with the properties of that caudillo." The justification for confiscation was written by the unitarian governor of Tucumán against the caudillo Felipe Ibarra: "The goods of Ibarra ought to be placed at our disposal to repair the damage which Ibarra has done to our countrymen."[13] According to Ernesto Quesada, the confiscatory practices of Rosas were much more moderate than those of the provincial caudillos. Whatever the truth of the rival propaganda claims, some of the consequences of confiscation were unforeseen.

Confiscation introduced an element of instability into the agrarian regime that had repercussions beyond the immediate victims. Property values were depressed; the market for land slumped, and estates changed hands at nominal prices, being sold under compulsion or from fear to partisans of the regime. Newcomers hesitated to take up ranching, and established estancieros refused to invest further, fearful of the future. The sense of insecurity was aggravated by the attack on estancia resources to supply the armies of Rosas. The appearance of a military patrol in search of supplies could mean disaster for an estanciero, as he saw his peons conscripted, his cattle commandeered, his horses driven away. And these exactions were taken from allies and neutrals as well as foes. Inevitably they had a depressing effect on landowners.

Insecurity for some was opportunity for others. Conditions turned to the advantage of foreigners, who were exempt from these national penalties and obligations. Rosas was scrupulous in his treatment of foreign nationals residing in the province, and they were virtually the only group that received the full protection of the law. Those who already held estates enjoyed a privileged position; others bought land cheaply, confident in the future. And freedom from local inheritance laws enabled them to dispose of their property as they wished. Thus did Rosas, otherwise acclaimed for conspicuous nationalism, promote foreign penetration of the Argentine economy. The circumstances were noticed by the English landowner Wilfrid Latham: "The protection which their 'treaties' secured to foreigners placed them under these circumstances at an advantage over the natives, inasmuch as the former were absolutely exempt from military service and from forced contribution, horses excepted, which were considered articles of war; and any injury to their properties, or the taking of their cattle in intestinal warfare, constituted claims for compensation under the existing treaties. Induced by the law price of land and the greater security which they enjoyed, foreigners, more especially the British, purchased largely of the lands offered for sale."[14] As Mansilla remarked, "You were lucky if you were English in those days." Tomás de Anchorena complained bitterly to Rosas of the favor shown to foreigners: "Your excessive generosity to gringos makes me very angry."[15] The truth is that comparable security and equal privilege were enjoyed by the close collaborators of Rosas, and the Anchorenas were the best example.

The structure erected by Rosas was appropriate for property concentration. According to the Cadastral Map of 1836, the large property, over 5,000 hectares (12,000 acres), was predominant, constituting 76.89 percent of holdings. Only 4.85 percent of holdings were under 2,500 hectares (6,000 acres). In the period 1830–1852 there were seventy-four holdings of over 15 square leagues (90,000 acres), and forty-two holdings of over 20 square leagues (120,000 acres). These were typically frontier estates. In the intermediate zone and the vicinity of Buenos Aires there was greater competition for land, a wider variety of holdings, the operation of a land market, and more rapid turnover of ownership. In general, size was important. Technology was primitive; the only criterion of success was the number of animals. There was no selection, no care, no special feeding, simply mass production of hides, tallow, grease, horns, and other products of the creole beasts. Return on investment was reputed to be upward of 30 percent per annum, though modern research in estancia account books "reveal[s] that normal profit margins in ranching and farming may not have been as high as the legendary 30 percent."[16]

In his will, written in 1862 in a relatively impoverished exile, Rosas claimed 78,544 pesos from the Anchorenas, "the price of my services and my expenses in their interest" during 1818–1830, when he established and administered for them various estancias.[17] The Rosas-Anchorena group did not acquire estancias for the sake of prestige or from an obsession with size; nor did they buy land on the margin of the economy or to leave it vacant. They were driven by ambition, a search for profit, and a taste for power, and their methods were strictly commercial. Their estates were situated in well-watered zones north of the Salado, where the countryside was fair and prosperous, the grass short and bright green and studded with beds of clover and thistle. They were models of industry and production, yielding up to the limit of their capacity. The Anchorenas were the largest landowners in the province, holding in 1830 in the names of Juan José and Nicolás alone approximately 134 square leagues, 200 square leagues in the name of the whole Anchorena group. Its holdings grew to 306 square leagues (1.836 million acres) by the 1840s.

Rosas, Proprietor

Rosas himself came some way behind the Anchorena in extent of estates. In the group of about seventeen landowners with property over 50 square leagues (300,000 acres), Rosas occupied tenth place with 70 square leagues (420,000 acres).[18] The total included land belonging to Rosas, Terrero and Company and was made up of various estancias, including Los Cerrillos, San Martín, and El Rey, together holding some 300,000 head of cattle. Apart from these he had land in Santa Fe. These were his holdings around 1830. Thereafter the extent of his property is difficult to calculate precisely. In addition to land accumulated by private enterprise, he also collected grants from the state. Throughout his life, he took the rewards for public service in the form of land. The most spectacular prize was the island of Choele Choel, granted to him by the assembly on June 6, 1834, after the Desert Campaign. He asked for this award to be commuted to an equivalent land grant of his own choice on the ground that the island was too important to leave the possession of the state. The equivalent calculated by Rosas was 50 square leagues, twice the size of the island; in the event the assembly voted him 60 square leagues of superior and more accessible cattle land in the province. In 1837, Rosas, Terrero and Company was liquidated by mutual agreement. The estancia San Martín and lands beyond the Salado went to Rosas; Terrero took Los Cerrillos. But this reorganization hardly affected the bulk of Rosas's lands, which lay outside the company's holdings. And if his estancias were on the grand scale, his urban estate was not inconsiderable.

Rosas had a large town property consisting of five houses in the calle Restaurador, which was part residential, part government offices. He also owned Palermo, a white stuccoed palace on the north side of Buenos Aires. Palermo was built on land acquired in 1836 and became his main residence; he later extended this estate, allegedly abusing his power to force neighbors to sell out and spending 4.6 million pesos of public money. This grandiose country house with its park surrounded by extensive iron railings, elaborate gardens, lake, stream, herd of ostriches, and orange groves was evidently expensive to build and maintain. It became one of the sights of Buenos Aires, impressing a number of travelers and observers. William MacCann was shown through the grounds by Rosas himself: "It might be asked, he said, why he built such a house on such a spot? He had built it for the purpose of contending against two great obstacles: the building was begun during the French blockade; as the people were then in a state of great excitement, he wished to calm down public opinion by a demonstration of confidence in a settled future; and by erecting his house on such an unfavourable site, he wished to give his countrymen an example of what could be done in overcoming obstacles, when there existed the will to do so."[19] No doubt these curious reasons occurred to Rosas in later tranquillity.

What was the final extent of this great property complex? In his will, Rosas specified certain claims that his heirs should make against the government of Buenos Aires for rightful compensation. He referred to "116,000 head of cattle, 40,000 sheep," which he had supplied to the government of Buenos Aires; then also "60,000 head of cattle, including cows, bullocks and calves, 1,000 prime steers, 3,000 fine horses, 100,000 sheep, 100,000 brood mares, and the rest of my property which the government has appropriated since February 2, 1852."[20] It would require vast estancias to support all this livestock; the official estimate was 136 square leagues (816,000 acres). How was this figure reached? By decree of February 16, 1852, the possessions of Rosas were declared public property because of his "bloody crimes." General Justo José de Urquiza later substituted another decree, ordering the existing property of Rosas to be handed over to Juan Nepomuceno Terrero, the exile's attorney. But the law of July 28, 1857, against the so-called *reo de lesa patria* ordered the sale of Rosas's lands on behalf of the legislature. Returns were made, an inventory was drawn up, but these did not indicate the dates or provenance of the various properties, only their extent. According to the Topographical Department (August 12, 1863), the total landed property "known as that of Rosas" amounted to 136 square leagues. The fiscal report of Dr. Pablo Cárdenas (November 23, 1863) gave a rather higher figure, 145 square leagues (870,000 acres).

Rosas not only accumulated land; he also exploited it. In his early years as an estanciero he laid down rules for his overseers and peons. From these, it can be inferred that he was not a progressive estanciero. He obtained results not by innovation but by work, organization, and meticulousness. He was less preoccupied with the quality of his animals than with their numbers. Unlike many estancieros, he does not appear to have tried to improve his stock by selective breeding. He did not specify the optimum number of animals for one *rodeo*. If his technology was deficient, however, his organization was impeccable, and in mobilizing labor, he had no equal. Charles Darwin met Rosas on the Desert Campaign in 1833 and was impressed by what he saw and heard: "He is a man of extraordinary character, and has a most predominant influence in the country, which it seems probable he will use to its prosperity and advancement. He is said to be the owner of seventy-four square leagues of land, and to have about three hundred thousand head of cattle. His estates are admirably managed, and are far more productive of corn than those of others. He first gained his celebrity by his laws for his own estancias, and by disciplining several hundred men, so as to resist with success the attacks of Indians." Darwin subsequently passed through Los Cerrillos, "one of the great estancias of General Rosas. It was fortified and of such an extent, that arriving in the dark I thought it was a town and fortress. In the morning we saw immense herds of cattle, the general here having seventy-four leagues of land."[21]

The estancia looked to the saladero as one of its principal outlets. Some estancieros produced for saladeros belonging to their own family group, which might also own warehouses in Buenos Aires or its own ships on the nearby coast. Others were in partnerships with saladeristas, as Rosas himself had once been. Otherwise a saladero would buy cattle direct from an independent estanciero or through an agent. The saladeros were large establishments where beasts were slaughtered, tallow extracted, flesh salted and dried, and hides prepared for export; the plant alone was a major investment and required careful management to yield a profit. By the 1840s their output had grown enormously, and each slaughtered some 200 to 400 animals a day during the season. The saladeros, therefore, were an integral part of the estancia system and as such they were favored by Rosas. In his annual message of 1849, he told the assembly that "these great establishments deserve the protection of the government, because they are factories which are vital to the national wealth."[22] In fact, they were easily the largest industry of Buenos Aires in terms of the number of people employed and the capital invested in them. The protection of which Rosas spoke consisted of virtual exemption from taxation. Financed and managed by experts, supplied by the estancias, favored by the government, the saladeros increased their output. The export value of jerked beef from Buenos Aires rose from 113,404 quintals (1,462,042 pesos) in 1835 to 198,046 (2,915,796) in 1841, a good year after the French blockade of 1838–1840, to 431,873 in 1851.

Rosas has been criticized for his failure to develop an integrated economic policy and to reconcile the divergent interests in the country. He favored the estancieros and cattle breeders at the expense of the small farmers and to the point that the country depended on imported grain. Yet there were compelling reasons for promoting the country's natural assets and encouraging its most successful exports even if this strategy meant diverting resources away from less profitable enterprises, worthy though they were. The agricultural colonization schemes of the 1820s failed through lack of capital, organization, security, and stability, in contrast to the great estancia expansion with its own internal dynamism. In any case, agriculture was subject to particular obstacles and needed special treatment. Labor was scarce and expensive, methods were primitive, and yield was low. The high cost of transport forced farmers to move nearer to cities, where land prices were higher; and there was always foreign competition. So agriculture needed capital and protection. At this point, governments hesitated, afraid of causing higher prices for food and alienating mass political supporters. Disillusioned by previous regimes, the farmers expected more from Rosas.

Rosas had some land under plough at Los Cerrillos, where he grew maize as well as raising cattle. Indeed, he was active in the grain trade, and it was alleged that through his agent Pablo Santillan, he cornered all the wheat of the province and sold it to the bakeries. There was arable farming near the outskirts of Buenos Aires, in districts to the north of the capital and also around Rosario. Rosas made a contribution toward further agricultural settlement, if only on a small scale. In 1832, he distributed *chacras,* or farms, in lots carved out of the lands of the old estancia of Nuestra Señora de Luján. These were given to settlers in the region, and they became active farms. Further farmlands were distributed during the Rosas administration, and by 1836 more than 200 settlers were benefiting from farm allocation.

After land itself, protection was what farmers most wanted from the government. Rosas was in a dilemma. He had to hold wheat and flour prices under control in order to prevent social unrest and political agitation. Such regulation meant keeping the door open to foreign imports and denying protection to the native farmers; and in the early 1830s, Rosas was concerned to stabilize domestic wheat prices, which fluctuated too sharply for comfort.

From 1834, however, farmers began to press more urgently for protection against foreign competition and for aid to improve the infrastructure of farming. At last, in December 1835 in the *ley de aduana* for 1836, Rosas gave judgment: he announced a policy of protection for industry and agriculture. National grain was protected by a moving tariff, and wheat imports were prohibited altogether when the domestic price of wheat fell below fifty pesos a *fanega*. There followed a modest recovery of farming and a series of good harvests; there was even some export of grain and flour, and various groups of farmers in different localities sent in votes of thanks for the new policy. The French blockade in 1839, however, disrupted these trends, as did the Anglo-French blockade of 1845–1847. Thereafter the government was silent on agriculture. The fact was that farmers were not a strong enough interest group economically or politically to sustain a campaign and draw a response.

The Pastoral Revolution

Whereas arable agriculture constituted no threat to the dominance of the cattle estancia, sheep farming did. The "merinization" of Buenos Aires, the rise of a substantial sheep and wool economy, began in the 1840s and led to a scramble for new land. The change was decisive for Argentina, for it was through the export of wool that the country first expanded its productive capacity, experienced capital accumulation, and hastened its integration into the world market.[23] Responding to international demand and the opportunities of comparative advantage, wool production and export became the main source of wealth. One of the reasons for the shift to sheep farming was that the price of wool rose not only faster than that of other agricultural products but, unlike hides and jerked beef, faster than inflation. The price index of wool rose from 100.0 in 1833 to 313.0 in 1850, compared with 158.2 for hides and 277.3 for jerked beef, a differential price rise due to demand from an expanding European textile industry. This demand provided a good export market and induced Argentine landowners to diversify into sheep. Many of the early sheep farmers were of English and Irish origin, and by the 1860s the British settlers had become some of the largest landowners in the country, although they were eventually outnumbered by native hacendados attracted by the high profits of sheep rearing. The state became interested once more in expanding the frontier, for although sheep did not require much labor, they needed a lot of land.

The growing interest in sheep breeding was reflected in imports of merinos from Europe and the United States; the creole and pampa sheep were also crossed with Saxony breeds. The number of improved sheep increased rapidly, and by the late 1840s the total number of sheep in the province of Buenos Aires was 6 million, of which one-third were improved breeds. Exports grew slowly. By 1836, wool represented 7.6 percent and cattle hides 68.4 percent of total exports from Buenos Aires; by 1851, wool was 10.3 percent and cattle hides were 64.9 percent of exports; by 1861, wool had increased to 35.9 percent, and cattle hides represented 33.5 percent. By 1852 the province had a stock of almost 10 million sheep, and wool exports were in the region of 25 million pounds.

A modern sheep industry required not only improved quality of sheep and more land but also innovations in the modes of production—better grasses, fenced fields, buildings for shearing and to house the wool, new wells, and clear ditches. All this improvement demanded more labor. The shepherd and the *puestero* were gradually replacing the gaucho and the *arriero*. Immigrant settlers began to arrive, either as hired laborers or as partners in profit-sharing enterprises or as tenant farmers. Between the 1840s and the 1860s sheep farms advanced at the expense of the estancia. The value of sheep increased tenfold, land values improved in the same ratio, there was now some subdivision of property, and land changed hands more frequently. Cattle estancias survived, of course, either as mixed farms or on low and marshy lands whose reedy grasses were unsuitable for sheep. Rosas himself had always encouraged sheep rearing, if not improvement, on his own estancias. But the original structure of estancia hegemony, so laboriously built since the 1820s, was to some extent undermined. There was now an alternative.

Rosas was a great hacendado, acting by instinct rather than theory, and the agrarian model that he favored was for the most part appropriate to the time and the place. The primitive estancia was correctly adjusted to Argentina in the first half of the nineteenth century; it corresponded to the facts of economic life and to the limits of available resources.[24] There was little hope of attracting large investment to change the economic structure at a time when foreign capital was in short supply and Argentina was a poor risk. Yet there was an abundance of empty land suitable for extensive development. The growth of the great estate extended the land frontier, improved the use of land, and harnessed the environment, and by specializing in ranching the estancia adapted itself to the chronic labor shortage. To concentrate on cattle breeding, moreover, was to produce an export commodity, or commodities, for which there was demand in the world market. It was not irrational to import cheap grain; given the paucity of the population, there was little need to encourage an expansion of agriculture. Even the land concentration occurred in circumstances that made disapprobation, if not irrelevant, at least exaggerated; estates were large not because a few rapacious people won the race for land or because marginal settlers were being evicted but because this was a vast and empty country where scale was totally different from that in Europe. Moreover, the insecurity of a fluctuating international market, especially for hides, favored the consolidation of cattle raising on an extensive scale, which required relatively low investments in technology and land and yielded very high profits. Investments had to be concentrated in cattle, and thus abundant, cheap, and relatively secure land was required. Rural pacification and low taxation levels for producers and merchants improved the advantages of nature and expanded livestock exports to the point that Buenos Aires had a favorable balance of trade. The result was the estancia, and there was some justification when Rosas claimed that land was the *negocio clásico*.

By the 1850s, however, the Rosas estancia was not simply classical; it was becoming archaic. There was a limit beyond which the Rosas economy could not grow. Lack of technology meant that the estancia could expand only by acquiring more and more land. It also specialized in a number of commodities—hides and jerked beef— for which overseas demand was limited, and in the slave markets of Brazil and Cuba, demand for these products was more likely to contract than to grow. In the final analysis, therefore, the Rosas system was economically stagnant. As Sarmiento remarked, everything was subordinated to cattle production: "Cows dictate Argentine policy! What are Rosas, Quiroga and Urquiza? Cowboys, nothing more."[25]

Had rosismo prevailed it would have held Argentina in an economic straitjacket. But the model was finally undermined from within, first by sheep farming, then by the agrarian revolution of the 1880s. Nevertheless, the Rosas regime left an indelible imprint on the agrarian structure of Argentina. The countryside was given its social and economic form before Argentina received its mass immigration, underwent a revolution on the pampas, and became a major exporter of grain and meat. Before modernization even began, the system of landholding, the size of estates, and in many cases the personnel had all been permanently implanted.

3

PATRÓN AND PEON

The Social Divide

The structure of society was simple and its scale was small. Argentina, so full of cattle, was empty of people, and even in the 1850s its population density was not much more than one inhabitant per square mile. Moreover, the population tended to extreme concentration; over one-third of the total was to be found in Buenos Aires and Córdoba. Yet Argentina underwent considerable demographic growth in the half-century following independence, as the official statistics show (see Table 3.1). The gap between 1825 and 1857 can be filled by the estimates of Diego de la Fuente, director of Argentina's first census (1869), who gives a total of 768,000 for 1839 and 935,000 for 1849. In the thirty-two years from 1825 to 1857, almost coterminous with the rule of Rosas, the population of Argentina roughly doubled itself. Growth was due essentially to a fall in the mortality rate in a period of improving conditions and freedom from major epidemics. There was only moderate immigration under

Table 3.1   Population Growth, Argentina 1800–1869

Year	Total
1800	300,000
1816	507,951
1825	570,000
1857	1,180,000
1869	1,736,923

Source: Data from Ernesto J. A. Maeder, *Evolución demográfica argentina de 1810 a 1869* (Buenos Aires, 1969), 22–26.

Rosas, though a number of Basques, French, Italians, and British entered Buenos Aires in the years between or after blockades.

The greatest population upswing was registered by the littoral provinces, which increased their share of the total from 36.0 percent in 1800 to 48.8 percent in 1869. Buenos Aires grew under Rosas but not spectacularly, and the historian of the period is dealing with a very small community. Rosas himself commissioned a census of the province in 1836; this was carried out successfully and gave a population of 62,228 for the city and 80,729 for the countryside, a total of 142,957 (see Table 3.2). The figures in Table 3.2 show that the countryside was steadily redressing the demographic balance as cattle and sheep farming drew increasing numbers to the rural sector. Official housing figures for Buenos Aires reflect the principal interruptions to economic activity, namely civil wars and blockades, but not the growth characteristic of a dynamic city.

The social structure was founded on land; it was the large estancia that conferred status and power. Among the eighty or so people who were members of the House of Representatives between 1835 and 1852, the assembly that voted Rosas into power and kept on voting for him, the majority (60 percent) were landowners or had occupations connected with land. The administration, too, was dominated by landowners. The closest political adviser of Rosas, Nicolás Anchorena, was the greatest landowner in the province, by 1852 having accumulated 306 square leagues (1,836,000 acres). Juan N. Terrero, economic adviser of Rosas, owned 42 square leagues (252,000 acres) and left a fortune of 53 million pesos. Angel Pacheco, Rosas's general, had 75 square leagues (450,000 acres).

Table 3.2   Province of Buenos Aires, Population 1797–1869

Year	City	Countryside	Total
1797	40,000	32,168	72,168
1822	55,416	63,230	118,646
1836	62,228	80,729	142,957
1855	90,076	183,861	273,937
1869	177,787	317,320	495,107

Source: Data from Ernesto J. A. Maeder, *Evolución demográfica argentina de 1810 a 1869* (Buenos Aires, 1969), 33–34.

Felipe Arana, minister of foreign affairs, had 42 square leagues. Even Vicente López, poet, deputy, and president of the high court, owned 12 square leagues (72,000 acres). At a local level, of course, power consisted only of land, and in the countryside landowners ruled all. As justices of the peace or military commanders, estancieros or their clients dominated local government. Often illiterate and usually ill educated, these authorities nevertheless possessed the essential qualifications of landownership and loyalty to Rosas and federalism. The rule of Rosas, therefore, saw the creation of a primitive ruling class in the countryside that was virtually the same as the local landed class; its members began by serving Rosas, but succeeding regimes, too, found them indispensable.

The polarization of society was absolute. There was an upper class of landowners and their associates and a lower class composing the rest of the population. There were some ambiguities, it is true, and some social margins were unclear. Both before and after the revolution for independence, commerce was economically important and socially respectable. In the Hispanic world wholesale trade had never been a barrier to social status, and in the Río de la Plata even retail trade was acceptable. There were many businesses situated in the center of Buenos Aires whose owners were the ancestors of some of the principal families of Argentina. But the urban elite of the early nineteenth century did not acquire a separate identity or become an independent middle class. Faced with insistent British competition in the years after independence, local businessmen began to divert their capital into land and become estancieros. There were no others to fill the middle ranks.

If there was little prospect of a native middle sector in the towns, there was even less chance of one emerging in the countryside, where an immense gulf separated the landed proprietor from the landless peon. It is true that there was a sizable group, perhaps one-third of the rural population of the province, that did not work directly on the land but found employment as traders, artisans, and carters or found delight in unemployment. But these were drawn into the prevailing polarization. William MacCann did not doubt that rural society was deeply divided: "There is as yet no middle class; the owners of land feeding immense flocks and herds form one class, their herdsmen and shepherds form another."[1] He thought that the immigrant farmers

were beginning to form an intermediate class of small flockhold-
ers, a variant of the English yeoman. This prospect was only par-
tially fulfilled, however, and in many cases the early immigrant
either dropped out or was integrated within a generation or two
into the estanciero class.

The homogeneity of this class was not absolute. Not all traders
were plebeians; not all estancieros were great landowners. Some were
owners of truly immense land concentrations, but there were some
whose estates were relatively modest. The former were often capital-
ists of urban origin with some education and aspirations to higher
standards of living. The latter were more likely to come from generations of country dwellers and were little removed in culture from
the gauchos around them—illiterate, indifferent to material com-
forts, and investing little in improvement. The difference between
the two was not entirely one of wealth. It was also determined by
cultural levels and social expectations. Sarmiento defined it in terms
of civilization and barbarism.

Yet in spite of differences in income, culture, and social style, the
estancieros were as one compared with the peons on their estates and
the gauchos on the pampas, and they had more in common with each
other than with the rest of society. There was a great deal of group
cohesion and solidarity among the landed class. Rosas himself was the
center of a vast kinship group based on land. He was surrounded by
a closely knit economic and political network linking deputies, law
officers, officials, and military who were also landowners and related
among themselves or with Rosas. Even when he was out of power and
far from Buenos Aires, he had considerable political influence
through Felipe Arana, the foreign minister; through his brother-in-
law Lucio N. Mansilla, the police chief; and especially through the
Anchorenas, his cousins and collaborators. Rosas used his extensive
patronage to bind this small oligarchy even closer. The Anchorenas in
particular were able to extend their urban and rural properties with
his direct assistance, making a profit from their alleged services to the
state. Rosas subsequently argued that as governor, he had advanced
their interests and increased their fortune immensely: "I served them
with notorious favoritism in everything they asked and needed."
Tomás de Anchorena thanked Rosas for exempting his son from military service and from mixing in the barracks with common people.
And Rosas himself admitted that he had deliberately exempted the

Anchorena estancias from state demands for peons, cattle, and horses, "a privilege which at that time was of supreme value to them."[2]

The values of the estanciero class were conservative, and most of them took it for granted that continuity was superior to change. Their social and in some cases their political ideas betrayed a basic affinity with the colonial order; for many of them the years before 1810 had indeed been a golden age, when in monopoly conditions their families had made their first fortunes. Tomás de Anchorena was such a type, though no doubt an extreme one. Friend, relation, and associate of Rosas, he lost no opportunity to extol the past and denounce novelty. His hostility to foreign influences amounted to xenophobia. In the House of Representatives in 1828, he fulminated against "that plague of corrupt foreigners which infests our countryside," arguing that the country had made more progress before the British invasion of the Río de la Plata in 1806 than afterward and that Rivadavia had admitted too many immigrants. He went on to claim an innate superiority in the prerevolutionary generation: "As far as enlightenment is concerned, I have observed, and no one will deny it, that generally the men of most capacity and credit in the country are those who were formed before the revolution and those whom these have since brought up in the old way." Men like this were opposed to the slightest modification of the colonial social structure. Tomás de Anchorena was a harsh opponent of social disturbance and subversion and a constant critic of anarchy and insecurity in the countryside, though even he had to admit, in his contemptuous way, that there was an order in the countryside that had not been changed: "The coarseness of our common people and country folk is not so striking as that of the same class in Europe. Although they lack manners, they are generally docile."

The views of Tomás de Anchorena were too extreme even for many of his elitist contemporaries, but his influence on Rosas was considerable. According to Mansilla, "Only one man, an Anchorena, had any real influence on him. And it was certainly not good for the country, though the person in question was a man of sound repute. But he belonged to the group of hacendados whose great remedy for everything was to prescribe a 'strong government.' "[3] Rosas depicted himself as removed from class interest, an honest man of the countryside called to restore the laws. In contrast, he expressed a social solidarity with his class that embraced even his political enemies: "I believed it important to accustom the people always to regard with respect the upper classes of the country *[las primeras categorías del pays]*, even those whose opinions differ from the prevailing ones. This is the reason why all my punishments were reserved for the scoundrels and rebels, for the whole pack of officials and ambitious leaders."[4]

Rosas was a man of conservative instincts, a creature of the colonial society in which he had been formed, a defender of authority and hierarchy. In spite of his overt populism, he stood for the preservation of the traditional social structure in its entirety. His political thinking was not profound, but it was consistent. His favorite model appears to have been the absolute monarchy of the old regime, his great aversion the spirit of revolution. He opposed change in Argentina and abhorred it in Europe. After 1852, pessimistic and powerless, he could only observe the events of contemporary history. In 1871, horrified by the advance of democracy, he wrote from Southampton: "When even the lower classes increasingly lose respect for law and order, and no longer fear divine punishment, only absolute powers are capable of imposing the laws of God and man, and respect for capital and its owners."[5] These are no doubt the views of conservative old age, influenced as much by convulsion in Europe as by change in Argentina, but they also summarize a lifelong philosophy.

Gauchos and Peons

At the end of the colonial period the pampas were inhabited by wild cattle, frontier Indians, and untamed gauchos. The gaucho was a product of race mixture; the components have been disputed, but there is no doubt that there were three races in the littoral: Indians, whites, and blacks. By simple definition the gaucho was a free man on horseback. But the term was used by contemporaries and by later historians to mean rural people in general. Yet many country people were neither gauchos nor peons; they were independent families living on small ranches or farms or earning a living in a pulpería or a village. Greater precision would distinguish between the sedentary rural dwellers working on the land for themselves or for their patrón and the pure gaucho, who was nomadic and independent, tied to no estate. Further refinement of terms would identify the *gaucho malo,* who lived by violence and near delinquency and whom the state regarded as a criminal. Sarmiento established his own typology: the Tracker, the Pathfinder, the Singer, the Outlaw. Whether good or bad, however, the classical gaucho asserted his freedom from all formal institutions; he was indifferent to government and its agents, indifferent to religion and the church. Social marginality for the gaucho was a desire as well as a condition. As Sarmiento observed, "He is happy in the midst of his poverty and privations," for he most valued complete independence and idleness.[6] He did not seek land; he lived by hunting, gambling, and fighting.

The nomadism of the gaucho had many social implications. It prevented settled work or occupation. Property, industry, land, habitation; these were alien concepts. So too was the gaucho family. The upper sector of society enjoyed great family stability and drew strength from ties of kinship. The lower sector was much weaker institutionally. The cultural division was partly an urban-rural one, but it was also a feature of the social structure. Whether we interpret it in terms of town and country, civilization and barbarism, or landowner and laborer, the difference in the degree of family stability was a fundamental feature of Argentine society. Among the gauchos and peons, unions were temporary, and families were only loosely joined. Marriage was the exception, and it was the unmarried mother who formed the nucleus of the rural family, for she was the only permanent parent, the one who kept together those homes that survived the rigors of rural life. Even if the father was not prone to gaucho nomadism, he usually did not have the economic resources to remain and sustain a family group; he had to sell his labor where he could, or else he was recruited into armies or montoneros. Lack of domesticity meant that the gauchos did not propagate themselves as a family group or preserve their identity through generations. Conditions were against them; they were cast adrift on the plains, homeless and hunted. The gauchos and the country folk in general were victims of government policy and the new economy: "Victims of the trimestrial levies for irregular warfare, they have no incentives to steady work and cannot, in fact, root themselves. At all times and by all parties they are hunted out, to fight or run away, disband or be disbanded, but to be hunted again; with none to share a home, with no home to be shared, driven to roam, they have no belongings and they do not propagate. What would it avail them to form homes or create surroundings as long as a press-gang incessantly dogs them, or they crouch and hide like hunted deer among dense scrub or thistle beds?"[7]

The ruling class in the countryside had traditionally imposed a system of coercion upon people whom they regarded as *mozos vagos y mal entretenidos,* vagabonds without employer or occupation, idlers who sat in groups singing to a guitar, drinking maté, gambling but apparently not working. This class was seen as a potential labor force and was therefore subject to all kinds of constraints and controls by the landed proprietors—the obligation to carry proof of identity and permits to leave the estancia, imprisonment, conscription to the Indian frontier, corporal punishment, and other penalties. The unfortunate gaucho might escape beyond the frontier, fleeing from crime or adversity, to become a *gaucho alzado;* but to live among the Indians was the worst possible stigma, signifying nonwhiteness, delinquency, and apostasy. No doubt there was much chronic lawlessness in the countryside and an identifiable criminal element: robbery of estancias, murder, gambling in pulperías, illicit sale of hides and other products, and traveling without a permit were not offenses invented by the authorities. However, legislators further sought to identify vagos y mal entretenidos as a criminal class by definition and vagrancy itself as a crime. In practice, to be poor, unemployed, and idle was equated with being a gaucho. The first object of the antivagrancy legislation was to impose law and order in the countryside; the second was to provide a labor pool for hacendados; the third, to produce conscripts for the army. The militia became, in effect, an open prison into which the most miserable part of the rural population was forcibly herded. By no stretch of the imagination were the rural militias spontaneous or popular forces.

For the gaucho the years after 1810 were, if anything, harsher than those before. During the colonial regime the free and nomadic gaucho traditionally had access to *cimarrones* (wild cattle) on the open range. But this tradition came to an end as the estancias were implanted and endowed and began to extend private property in the pampas and appropriate all cattle to themselves. Now the landowners, with the support of republican governments, began to prevent illicit hunting, slaughter, and trade in hides and to defend their land and cattle. There was a prolonged struggle between the hacendado and the gaucho. In times of turbulence and civil war the marginal people of the countryside revived the communal practices of the past and once more took cattle, but when order returned, the hacendados reaffirmed the rights of property. This did not mean that cimarrones no longer roamed the range. Now the peons of the estancia, not free gauchos, caught the wild cattle and took them to their masters; otherwise such appropriation was rustling.

Coercive controls and the horror of life among the Indians drove the gaucho into the hands of the hacendado, but as a hired ranch hand, a wage earner, a *peón de estancia*. It is true that labor scarcity gave the peon some advantage, and an active labor market and job mobility coexisted with repressive rural codes; at the same time, collaboration between estancieros and army deserters resolved many of the problems of labor shortage. The rural regime was not entirely unfair toward the worker, and on many estancias it provided a stable living and job security if that was what the laborer wanted. But for the gaucho the price was still loss of freedom. He became virtually the property of his patrón; if the estate was his sanctuary, it was also his prison. An estanciero needed personal as well as institutional power. He had to be as tough and talented a gaucho as his own peons, if not more so. He had to have enough skill and resources to beat the Indians and to resist the authorities if necessary. He had to be a fighter as well as a proprietor, a man who could protect as well as employ.

The relation of patron and client was the essential bond, based on a personal exchange of assets between these unequal partners. The landowner wanted labor, loyalty, and service in peace and war. The peon wanted subsistence and security. The estanciero, therefore, was a protector, the possessor of sufficient power to defend his dependants against marauding bands, recruiting sergeants, and rival hordes. He was also a provider who developed and defended local resources and could give employment, food, and shelter. Thus a patrón recruited a *peonada* that followed him blindly in ranching, politics, and war. These individual alliances were extended into a social pyramid as patróns in turn became clients to more powerful men until the peak of power was reached and they all became clients of a superpatron, the caudillo. Rosas was the archetypal caudillo, the embodiment of personal power in a society that responded to patronage rather than politics.

Rosas: Populist or Patrician?

Did Rosas have a mass following among the gauchos? Was he a true populist? Did he, as contemporaries implied and historians asserted, represent the rural masses against the urban elites? Rosas's view of the popular classes was conditioned by his economic interests and social position. It was a predictably conservative and authoritarian view but was based not on an attitude of cruelty or contempt but, in the beginning, on apprehension. Soon after taking possession of his estancia Los Cerrillos, he wrote to the government in 1817, complaining of the terrifying insecurity and anarchy in the region of Monte, which was infested by hordes of vagrants, idlers, and delinquents who respected neither property nor persons but who insolently roamed the countryside defying the authority of magistrates and landowners alike: "Only a month ago I was attacked in my own estancia because I tried to stop ostrich hunting, in which dozens of men helped themselves to my animals. I had to defend myself in a knife attack; and since then my life depends on striking back at idlers and delinquents."[8]

The gaucho as delinquent was a familiar interpretation. It was the lawlessness of the countryside that first impressed Rosas. And this vivid awareness of incipient anarchy bred in him a determination to conquer it, first in his own environment, then in the political world beyond. There was a period, in the late 1820s, when he seems to have genuinely feared an autonomous movement of protest from below, a movement that he sought to capture and control. This is the context in which occurred his often cited interview with the Uruguayan envoy, Santiago Vázquez, on the day after he took office as governor in December 1829. Then he claimed that unlike his predecessors, he had cultivated the people *"de las clases bajas"* and had gaucherized himself in order to control them. Previous governments, he argued,

> acted very well towards educated people, but they despised the lower
> classes, the country people, the men of action. . . . It seemed to me that

in the crisis of the revolution the governing parties would be displaced by the lower class who would impose their rule and cause worse evils. As you know, the dispossessed are always inclined against the rich and the powerful. So from then onwards I thought it very important to gain a decisive influence over this class in order to control it and direct it; and I was determined to acquire this influence at all costs. I had to work at it relentlessly, sacrificing my comfort and fortune, in order to become a gaucho like them, to speak like them, to do everything they did. I had to protect them, represent them, guard their interests. In short I had to spare no effort, neglect no means to secure their allegiance.[9]

Rosas, therefore, identified culturally with the gaucho. He brought up his son to feel the same. Rosas's idea of a joke while riding with his followers was to lasso a man suddenly round the neck, pull him off his horse, and drag him along for a distance. The crude and obscene jokes, the presence of a court jester, Eusebio, and the violent horseplay and clowning all displayed what one observer described as "su genio y carácter gauchesco."[10] Some of this behavior had a positive effect. Charles Darwin evidently heard the stories current about Rosas's gaucho sympathies and talents and could see that even his iron discipline drew a grudging respect from his men. He was impressed by his horsemanship and all-round proficiency in rural ways: "By these means, and by conforming to the dress and habits of the Gauchos, he has obtained an unbounded popularity in the country, and in consequence a despotic power."[11] Darwin was further struck by a certain egalitarianism in Rosas's social relations. Rosas's enemies made much the same point, though with bitter disapproval. According to Andrés Lamas, a spokesman for the émigrés in Montevideo, Rosas was a social danger who took from the rich and gave to the "vicious and idle," basing his power exclusively on the ill-educated and "brutalized part of society," giving handouts to the lower orders, allowing them to take revenge on their superiors, and in general applying a policy of deep social divisiveness.[12]

To identify culturally with the people of the country was not the same thing as uniting with them socially. To behave like a gaucho was not necessarily to represent or elevate or save the gaucho. Subsequent rosista historiography claimed that Rosas identified totally with the gauchos and that they rose spontaneously for him. A number of contemporary observers spoke in the same way. The British ministers invariably reported that the lower classes of town and country supported Rosas, and they gave the impression of gaucho hordes riding to the capital in the cause of their savior. Philip Yorke Gore reported: "The Gauchos, or inhabitants of the country districts, are ardently attached to General Rosas, to whom, as their acknowledged chief and benefactor, they have long looked up with an incredible devotion." Rosas himself explained to John Henry Mandeville that "there is no aristocracy here to support a government, public opinion and the masses govern." Henry Southern believed, "It is the secret of his power that he taught the Gaucho of the plains that he was the true master of the towns. It was on the basis of troops of his own cattle-breeders and drivers and horse tamers that he first established his authority which he has maintained to this day by a cunning and dextrous use of the same arm."[13]

These impressions, however, are distorted or at least open to misinterpretation. In the first place, the core of Rosas's forces were his own peons and dependants, who had to follow him in war as they worked for him in peace. Who were Rosas's peons? They were composed, first, of gauchos, previously "wild" and nomadic, now tamed and tied to his estancia, where they worked as ranch hands in return for pay and protection. Second, they included "friendly" Indians. Some of these worked for him as peons; others simply lived in the zones near his estancias or camped on his land, collaborating with him against incursions of enemy Indians or against political foes in return for the patronage of a powerful caudillo who impressed them and spoke their language. Third, the Rosas estancias harbored a number of outlaws. He deliberately recruited delinquents, deserters from the army, escaped prisoners, and encouraged them to seek refuge on his estates, partly as a response to the labor shortage, partly as a control measure against anarchy. Rosas, of course, did not tolerate offenses against property. As Sarmiento pointed out, he made his estancia "a sort of asylum for murderers," but as a landed proprietor, he did not extend his protection to robbers.[14] Otherwise he cast his net fairly widely, as General La Madrid noted: "In spite of the severity with which he forced them to obey, Rosas was the hacendado who had most peons, because he paid them well and joined in their horse-play during breaks from work, and he patronized all the villains and deserters who made for his estancias and no one could touch them."[15] Gauchos, Indians, delinquents, whoever they were, Rosas's peons were his servants rather than his supporters, his clients rather than his allies. When Rosas said to his gauchos "Adelante!" it was an order, not a political speech.

These surges of the rural population, moreover, occurred in times of exceptional crisis, rebellion, or war, such as in 1829, 1833, and 1839. In 1828–1829, as has been seen, Rosas deliberately exploited rural unrest to assemble popular forces to counter the unitarian rebellion.[16] One who knew him then reported: "He established a camp, which had all the privileges of a sanctuary, for every malefactor, in every district from Buenos Ayres to Upper Peru."[17] He used these marginal elements as part of his "popular forces." In 1833, waiting in the wings during the Desert Campaign, he instructed his wife to cultivate the poor as a base for a political comeback: "You have already observed how valuable is the friendship of the poor and therefore how important it is to cultivate it and not to lose any opportunity of attracting and keeping their sympathies. So do not lose contact. Write to them frequently; send them gifts and do not worry about the cost. I say the same about the mothers and wives of the pardos and coloreds who are loyal. Do not hesitate to visit those who are worth it and to take them on outings in the country, also assist them as far as you can when they are in trouble."[18] And Doña Encarnación, agent of rosismo, "heroine of the federation," patronized the popular elements and the people of color, calling in black women to receive her favor, sending them out as clients. Her patio was like a club for the populace. Rather than politicization, this was a primitive and personalist form of political manipulation. There was no organization: Rosas, his wife, and a few friends held all the strings.

On all these occasions when Rosas needed to make a critical political push, he enlisted the gauchos in the countryside and the mob in the city. They were the only manpower available, and for the moment they had a value outside the estancia. The normal agrarian regime however, was very different. And as Sarmiento pointed out, the gaucho forces lasted only as long as Rosas needed them. Once Rosas had the apparatus of the state in his possession, from 1835, once he controlled the bureaucracy, the police, the *mazorca,* or paramilitary squads, and above all the regular army, he did not need or want the popular forces of the countryside. He recruited, equipped, armed, and purged an army of the line, detachments of which were used *against* the countryside to round

88888

up the levies. It was the army camped at Santos Lugares that gave
him his ultimate power.

The gaucho militias, furthermore, were popular forces only in
the sense that they were composed of the peons of the countryside.
They were not always volunteers for a cause; nor were they politi-
cized. Methods of military recruitment in general were crude and
often violent. The British minister, William Gore Ouseley, took a
cynical view of spontaneity. He described the brutal activities of
General Prudencio Rosas while raising levies in a village near Buenos
Aires, where he gave a man 200 lashes for remonstrating against
forced conscription. The severity of the punishment killed the man,
but General Rosas thought it set a good example. "This mode of
raising troops," commented Ouseley, "is described in late numbers
of the *Gaceta* as the 'spontaneous and enthusiastic rising of the people in their own defence against the aggressions of the savage
Unitarians.' "[19] As for the militias, they were officered and led by the
justices of the peace, by regular army commanders, and by
estancieros. The fact of belonging to a military organization did not
give the peons political power or representation, for the rigid structure of the estancia was also built into the militia, where the
estancieros were the commanders, their overseers the officers, and
their peons the troops. These troops did not enter into direct relations with Rosas; they were mobilized by their patrón, which meant
that Rosas received his support not from free gaucho hordes but
from estancieros leading their peon conscripts, a service for which
the estancieros were paid by the state. Rosas himself was from the
beginning the most powerful estanciero, and his peonada was the
most numerous and best equipped. But that did not make him a
populist leader.

Even the use of the word "gaucho" was ambiguous in rosista ter-
minology. It had two meanings, according to the situation. In public, it was used as a term of esteem and perpetuated the idea that the
gaucho, like the estanciero, was a model of native virtues and that
the interests of both were identical. Rosas, too, helped to propagate
the myth that the estanciero understood the gaucho and was concerned only with his welfare; this was one of the themes of the dictator's propaganda and was incorporated into popular songs of the
times. In private, however, especially in police usage, "gaucho"
meant "vago, mal entretenido, delinquent." The first usage repre-

sented political propaganda. The pejorative meaning expressed class distinction, social prejudices, and economic attitudes; it was used by the landowner, short of labor, confronting the countryman who wished to remain free. According to William MacCann, "The term Gaucho is one offensive to the mass of the people, being understood to mean a person who has no local habitation, but lives a nomadic life; therefore in speaking of the poorer classes I avoid that term."[20]

The poorer people, of course, were a heterogeneous group, not a unified class. They were peons on estancias, dependants subject to a patrón, free laborers, farmers and tenants, small ranchers, and the marginal population that was almost professional montoneros. Uneducated, illiterate, ignorant of public issues, these groups could not participate in even the crudest political process; they were incapable of autonomous action, of organizing themselves, or of responding to political leadership. The history of populism, of course, contains many examples of leaders who offer benefits to apolitical masses without necessarily incorporating them into politics or basically changing society. Did Rosas do this? Did he improve conditions for the rural population? Did he deliver economic and social benefits?

The domination of the economy by the estancia was continued and completed under Rosas, as has been seen. No land was granted to the gaucho; no property was allocated to the peon. It is sometimes argued that under Rosas the rural laborers were free men, respected and defended; yet there is no evidence that Rosas ever queried the existing social structure. He inherited from previous regimes a discriminatory social legislation and a political system designed to exclude participation. The electoral law of August 14, 1821, which remained in force throughout the rule of Rosas and beyond, established direct elections and universal male suffrage; all free men from the age of twenty had the right to vote, and all property owners over twenty-five had the right to be candidates for election. This was the law, and there were no literacy or property qualifications for voters. But in practice the illiterate gauchos could not vote as free men. The system was a fraud and a farce: the government sent a list of official candidates, and it was the task of the justices of the peace to ensure that these were elected. Open and verbal voting, the right of the justices to exclude voters and candidates whom they considered unqualified, the intimidation of opposition; these and many other malpractices reduced the elections to absurdity. Rosas frankly admitted that elections had to be controlled, and he condemned as hypocrisy the demand for free elections. His government, he told the assembly in 1837, "has sent many worthy residents and magistrates throughout the province lists which contained the names of those citizens who in its opinion were fit to represent the rights of their country, in order to favor their election, if so they wished."[21] In practice the Rosas lists were an absolute order, and those gauchos who went to the polls did so as voting fodder.

The politically defenseless gaucho was attacked on all sides by harsh labor laws that classified as a vagrant anyone who did not have a recognized employment or occupation endorsed by an employer. To inhabit or to move about the provincial territory, a man had to have a *papeleta de conchabo,* a certificate stating that he was working for a known proprietor and, if he was on the move, the date when he would return to his usual place of work. If he was found without this certificate, he was considered a vagrant and liable to be arrested and sent to the army. In this way the gaucho lost his freedom and civil rights and became a peon dependent utterly on a patrón; if he wanted to keep out of the army or prison, there was only the estancia. The only individuality the peon retained was his particular occupation on the estancia, and some were more skilled than others. Thus the estancia became a closed sociopolitical reserve in which the peon had no rights.

The severity of these sanctions reflected the emptiness of the pampas, the very low population density, and the ruthless search for labor in a period of estancia expansion. For these reasons, Rosas could not be expected basically to alter the discriminatory legislation that he inherited. He simply elucidated the law, defining more precisely the crime and the punishment of vagrants, robbers, deserters, and other delinquents without granting the poorer classes any means of legal defense. If anything, the application of the law became harsher, and there was a tendency toward shortening criminal proceedings. Rosas continued to apply the existing regulations against vagrancy, and although his local conscription levies simply continued from previous administrations, the incidence of recruitment increased as his wars increased. In 1830, he decreed that militiamen could not travel about the country without their documents duly signed by the local magistrate. A militiaman could not change domicile without permission and without informing his commanding officer. In his speech at the beginning of the legislative session of 1836, he reported the strong action taken against vagos y mal entretenidos and the increased numbers conscripted into the forces. Corporal punishment in the army was severe; the recruits were virtual prisoners, kept under guard until the actual moment of marching; and the army canteens and pulperías robbed them of their small allowances. Conscription was not the only punishment for rural delinquency. The lash and various forms of torture, punishments characteristic of the colonial past, were continued beyond independence and into the Rosas regime. On the estancias, proprietors still punished their peons by putting them in stocks or staking them out like hides in the sun. It was a seigneurial regime in which the peons were deprived of full civil rights and the countryside was ruled by an informal alliance of estancieros and militia commanders who were often the same people. They were joined by a third oppressor.

The key agent of control in the countryside was the justice of the peace. The office was established in 1821 to fill the gap left by the suppression of the colonial *cabildo,* but its original judicial and administrative functions in a given district were soon extended to include those of commander of militia, police chief, and tax collector. In a sense the office grew up with the estancia. In the years after 1821 the colonization of the empty countryside was accompanied by the creation of a new officialdom, and it became a convenient instrument of caudillo rule. The justice of the peace was not a constitutional official but a political agent, a servant of state centralism. Rosas was quick to see this advantage, and he took control of the justices in the campaign of 1829; from then on they were his creatures. He scrutinized their appointment and monitored their every action. "From an administrative point of view, Rosas regarded the countryside as an immense estancia, divided into stations; in charge of each was a justice of the peace, a kind of feudal lord dependent upon the seigneurial power established in the capital."[22]

The justices both administered the rural labor laws and policed the population; they pursued criminals, deserters, and vagrants; they reported on properties and their owners, and also on their political affiliations; they took censuses of the population, applied confiscations of property, presided over elections. Yet in general the administration of justice was defective, and there was a kind of official delinquency just as bloodthirsty as gaucho delinquency. Most justices of the peace were uneducated and ill qualified for their office; some were totally illiterate. No doubt there were exceptions, a few worthy officials who tried to shield their districts from the worst excesses of government power and to protect individuals from political vengeance. But in general the justices of the peace were either willing accomplices or helpless instruments of a policy expressed in arrests, confiscations, conscriptions, or worse and directed against anyone who could be branded a unitarian or delinquent.

Some observers, however, were impressed by the rough justice administered in the province and by the law and order imposed by Rosas. The crime rate appeared to have dropped, personal security to have improved, property to be better protected. The evidence, moreover, comes at different times from various sources, some of them British: "Since Rosas's administration there has been little to fear from them [the gauchos]: I do not say that their love of plunder, the natural propensity of a savage, is extinct among them: but as the Captain General invariably shoots them, or makes them food for powder by making soldiers of them if they indulge in this propensity, a robbery, to my knowledge, by violence, is unknown."[23] This observation was made in the mid-1830s. A decade later William MacCann observed on the security of even remote properties since Rosas had established the rule of law in the pampas: "I have been assured that such was not the case before the ascendancy of General Rosas; but it being well known that, owing to the system of police established under his government, all, whether rich or poor, who were implicated in the violation of the established laws of the country were sure to suffer the extreme penalty of their crimes, robbery and outrage are almost unknown."[24]

This was the classic defense of Rosas, that his rule was the only alternative to anarchy; it was propagated by Rosas himself, and it particularly appealed to foreigners. But not to all of them. A French observer had other views: "In the Argentine pampas there are men more dreadful than the bad gaucho and who do more harm, without however being forced to flee from the law, because they themselves represent lawful authority and justice. They are the officials honored by Rosas with his favor and confidence: the military commanders of the countryside and the justices of the peace."[25]

Rosas and the Blacks

In spite of the May Revolution, the liberal declarations of 1810, and the subsequent hope of social as well as political emancipation, slavery survived in Argentina, fed by an illegal slave trade. The *trata de negros* of the eighteenth century had produced a sizable slave population, most of it employed in domestic service or the artisan industries. The abolition of the slave trade within the United Provinces by decrees of April 9 and May 14, 1812, reduced the source of supply; and the treaty of February 2, 1825, with Great Britain obliged the United Provinces to cooperate with Britain in the total suppression of the slave trade. The abolition of slavery itself, however, involving as it did rights of property and scarce labor, was more difficult to achieve, and the institution long survived the May Revolution.

At the end of the colonial period the Río de la Plata contained about 30,000 slaves out of a population of 400,000, or about 8 percent. The incidence of slavery was greatest in the towns, and after 1810 the people of color continued to concentrate in Buenos Aires. A breakdown of the population in Buenos Aires from 1810 to 1838 appears in Table 3.3. In 1810 there were 11,837 blacks and mulattos in Buenos Aires, or 29.3 percent of the total population of 40,398, and over 77 percent of the blacks were slaves. In 1822, of the 55,416 inhabitants of the city of Buenos Aires, 13,685, or 24.7 percent, were blacks and mulattos; of these, 6,611, or 48.3 percent, were slaves. In 1838, people of color constituted 14,928 out of 62,957, or 23.71 percent.

Although slave numbers declined, slavery survived and an internal slave trade continued to function. A number of upper-class families held slaves and valued them as status symbols in the home and as laborers on the land. Rosas was a slave owner. The vast acquisition of lands, the exploitation of growing estancias, the increased production for saladeros, all raised the demand for labor at a time when peons were scarce and military recruitment was heavy during the war with Brazil. Rosas bought slaves for himself and the Anchorenas. In the period 1816–1822, he acquired three slaves in Santa Fe; the Anchorenas bought three also. In 1822–1823, Rosas bought fifteen slaves for Anchorena estancias, and in 1828, he made further purchases. On the estancias Los Cerrillos and San Martín alone he had

Table 3.3   Black and Mulatto Population, Buenos Aires, 1810–1838

	1810		1822		1836		1838	
	Number	Percent	Number	Percent	Number	Percent	Number	Percent
Whites	28,116	69.6	40,616	73.3	42,445	67.34	42,312	67.2
Blacks and mulattos	11,837	29.3	13,685	24.7	14,906	23.65	14,928	23.71
Indians and mestizos	192	0.5	1,115	2.0				
Foreigners and others	253	0.6			4,019	6.37	3,649	
Troops					1,665	2.63	2,068	3.28
Total	40,398	100.0	55,416	100.0	63,035	99.99	62,957	

Source: Data from Marta B. Goldberg, "La población negra y mulata de la ciudad de Buenos Aires, 1810–1840," *Desarrollo Económico,* 16, no. 61 (1976), 75–99.

thirty-four slaves. He was severe in his treatment of slaves, and he favored the lash to keep them obedient and preserve social order.

Rosas was responsible for a partial revival of the slave trade. His decree of October 15, 1831, allowed the sale of slaves imported as servants by foreigners "in order to allow the unfortunate children of Africa to experience the benefits of civilization" and also, evidently, to relieve the shortage of labor. Apart from slavery allowed under this decree, during the 1830s, slaves continued to be illegally brought into the country from Brazil, Uruguay, and Africa. The government did not seriously challenge this trade. Rosas himself argued that slavery was necessary to supply labor for the estancias, industries, and households. Throughout the 1830s, newspapers daily carried advertisements offering slaves for sale. According to British observers, slaves were "sold with little concealment."[26] The British government pressed Rosas for action and in particular sought an anti–slave trade treaty but received no response until Rosas needed British support against the French blockade of 1838. A comprehensive anti–slave trade treaty was signed on May 24, 1839, providing for reciprocal search, mixed courts, and claims procedures. By 1843, according to a British estimate, there were no more than 300 slaves in the Argentine provinces, though the coloreds formed one-fourteenth of the total population.

Some slaves regarded Rosas as an escape route, a means of emancipation, which is evidence of the esteem in which he was held.
Fugitive slaves from Brazilian vessels made their way to the headquarters of Rosas to petition for their freedom. Foreign slave owners
in Buenos Aires were particularly liable to lose their slaves. A U.S. citizen, Andrew Thorndike, appealing to rights of private property and
the absence of a decree of abolition, petitioned Rosas for the return
of a freed slave who had cost him 1,200 pesos.[27] He appealed in vain.
Meanwhile, the traditional avenues of emancipation were still open:
slaves who joined the federalist army, especially if they belonged to
unitarian owners, gained freedom in return for military service. A
French factory owner petitioned Rosas for the return of one of his
slaves who had made his way to Santos Lugares and enlisted; the
owner obtained neither his return nor financial compensation.[28]
Emancipation appears to have increased toward the end of the
regime: "It is already well known in Brazil that if a slave can once
reach the territory of the Confederation, he is free. Rosas has been
here the Liberator of the African, and if he is looked to with affection by any class in the state, it is by the dark coloured races, whom
he has invariably favoured."[29] When, in the Constitution of 1853,
slavery was finally abolished in the whole of Argentina, there were
few slaves left.

The opposition attacked Rosas's record on slavery, and
inevitably the liberals in Montevideo made much of the issue. They
contrasted the policy of the old republic after the May Revolution
with what followed under Rosas: "He issued a decree, eight years
ago, allowing negro slaves to be brought in, because he and the
Anchorenas needed them for their estancias."[30] Juan Bautista Alberdi
also criticized the discrimination practiced against people of color,
though he referred to the whole of the Río de la Plata and not only
to the Rosas state. He cited the expulsion of four young blacks from
a café in Montevideo in 1840. The theater was also closed to blacks.
But racism of this kind was never a feature of Rosas's personal attitude toward blacks and mulattos, which was crudely friendly.

Rosas had many blacks in his employment and many more in
his political service. He did not raise them socially, but neither did
he discriminate against them racially. They had an accepted place in
his household, and outside his immediate circle, they gave him useful support in the streets and were part of his "popular" following.

The blacks of Buenos Aires were grouped in various societies, such as the Sociedad Conga or the Nación Banguela, each with its own name, leaders, and distinctive dress, the whole having a strong and relatively recent African character. On the outskirts of the city, they formed a series of small communities, black enclaves where they preserved their dances, music, customs, and language. Rosas patronized some of their festive gatherings and discreetly attended their *candombes*, as did his daughter, Manuela.

The blacks in turn gave Rosas their blind support. They joined the popular classes as they flocked to the Carnival of Rosas, where they beat their drums, marched, danced, and shouted in a delirium of drink and excitement, "Viva el Restaurador!" These orgies of drinking, dancing, and fighting were a sardonic hint to the upper classes of the tumult they could expect without a strong restraining hand. More particularly the regime used the blacks and mulattos for two purposes. They were deployed in a military role in Buenos Aires and the province, where they formed a militia unit, the *negrada federal*, black troops in red shirts, many of them former slaves. Rosas also used them as political tools. When, from the Desert Campaign in August 1833, he directed political activity in Buenos Aires, he advised his wife and other agents to identify the opposition in the army by observing officers' wives and their contacts, recommending in effect a spying system in which slaves and blacks were encouraged to report on their masters and mistresses. The black Domiciano, a former peon on Rosas's estancia, was one of the chief cutthroats in the antiunitarian squads. Yet in the final analysis the demagogy of Rosas among the blacks and mulattos did nothing to alter their position in the society around them.

Society took its form under Rosas and endured beyond his regime. The dominance of the landowners, the abasement of the gauchos, and the dependence of the peons were all the heritage of the Rosas years. Argentina bore the imprint of extreme stratification for many generations to come. Society became set in a rigid mold to which economic modernization and political change later had to adapt. Rosas was to some extent a creature of the class structure, a product of the landowning elite, a man formed in the social image of the estancia. But he was not simply a social phenomenon; he was idiosyncratic. He did more than inherit a system; he helped to create a society. Beginning with the estancia, he established values and structures that permeated the whole province and became the lifeblood of the Rosas state. In the estancia, he was an absolute ruler, and from his peons he demanded unqualified obedience. At the very outset, he punished his men mercilessly. The penalty for carrying a knife on Sundays and holidays was two hours in the stocks, for other misdemeanors a staking out, for going to work without a lasso fifty lashes on the bare back. He always insisted on undergoing the same discipline himself, ordering his servant to administer the prescribed punishment to him as an example and in turn punishing those who hesitated to chastise their own master. This grim eccentricity impressed society by its results: "This was the way Rosas began to acquire a reputation. In the southern countryside in particular there was more obedience to his orders than to those of the government itself."[31]

The Rosas system was a product of environment and idiosyncrasy. His state was the estancia writ large. Society itself was built upon the patrón-peon relationship. Rosas helped to define the terms of this relationship, working on a state of nature where life was brutish and property at risk. "Subordination" was his favorite word, authority his ideal, order his achievement. As a British minister spoke of Rosas at the peak of his power, "He praises the lower orders as docile and obedient."[32] In the beginning, obedience was not so assured. Indeed, Rosas explained the origins of his regime as a desperate alternative to anarchy:

> Society was in a state of utter dissolution: gone was the influence of those men who in every society are destined to take control; the spirit of insubordination had spread and taken widespread roots; everyone knew his own helplessness and that of others; no one was prepared either to order or to obey. In the countryside there was no security for lives or property. . . . The inevitable time had arrived when it was necessary to exercise personal influence on the masses to re-establish order, security, and laws; and whatever influence on them the present governor had, he was greatly tormented, because he knew the absolute lack of government resources to reorganise society.[33]

The rationale of the regime, its origin, and its development would have been instantly recognizable to Thomas Hobbes.

4

AN ALTERNATIVE ARGENTINA

Urban Society

Buenos Aires was a port as well as a province, and within its streets and squares between the river and the plains there was a life and society appropriate to a city. A small but discernible middle group existed in spite of social polarization. Even in the countryside there were modest ranchers, tenant farmers, overseers, storekeepers, all dependent in one form or another on the great rural proprietors but possessing a status superior to the propertyless peons. Nearer to the city lived the *chacareros,* the suburban farmers and market gardeners, and within its environs lived the employees of the *mataderos,* or slaughterhouses. Personnel of the service sector were active in the port—servants, porters, coachmen, carters, laundresses—most of them at the bottom of society, many of them blacks and mulattos, and a few aspiring to higher things. Bureaucrats, the liberal professionals, police, military staff, and churchmen were all recognizable city dwellers occupying various social positions. So were the urban artisans, owners or employees of workshops, makers of manufactured goods or processed products for the local market, and contractors and workers in the construction industry. Finally, the merchants were an important urban group, to some extent a foreign enclave but including local families even at the top as well as in the retail trade and in clerical and other minor posts. All these types differed widely among themselves in income and interests, but they had a common identity in their urban or near-urban occupation and residence. Some of them sought a political voice and protection against other interests.

Although Buenos Aires was in many respects a rural rather than an urban society, selling or exporting the products of an exclusively

pastoral economy, it still contained the traditional artisan industries, whose owners and workers were an integral part of the urban
structure. Artisan groups had established their identity in colonial
society, though by 1810 they had failed to secure a high status. Yet
artisan industry survived the transition to independence and the
foreign competition to which it was now exposed; the wars of independence gave added impetus to many existing industries, and a
new sector that processed livestock products was about to develop.
The industrial sector was capable of producing some import substi-
tution when necessary, as during the war with Brazil and the consequent blockade.

Argentina, of course, did not undergo an industrial revolution at
this time, and there was no transformation from one mode of production to another. The historian will look in vain for evidence of
specialization and division of labor, the application of technology
and mechanical power, and efficient methods of minimizing unit
costs and maximizing returns. It is obvious that preconditions for
industrialization did not exist. Although the economy had an export
sector, it was not dynamic enough to generate surplus capital for
investment; the only possible exception was the saladero, which was
financed by a mixture of internal savings and foreign capital. In general, foreign investment was not attracted to traditional industries.
Finally, the internal market was not yet developed; the total population was small, the consumer population smaller still, and neither
was increasing rapidly enough to stimulate industrial production.
Industry remained, therefore, at the artisan and workshop level.
Quality of product was usually low, technology primitive, the market limited, the labor force small and, in the interior provinces, scattered around the countryside in domestic units rather than grouped
in larger concentrations.

In Buenos Aires, however, the scale of operations was greater and
the numbers engaged were larger. There were numerous establishments for the manufacture of clothing, uniforms, leatherware, shoes,
hats, silverware, vehicles, furniture, and building materials as well as
for the processing of foodstuffs and beverages. An official census of
1836 listed a total of 121 "factories."[1] In the next twenty years
industry made some advance through the application of new
machinery and the growth of labor specialization. By 1853 there
were probably six to eight steam engines operating in Buenos Aires,

some in flourmills, others in soap factories. Such progress as was made, however, did not signify true industrialization. It was in the saladeros that a combination of steam power and division of labor led to increased output and variety of product. But the saladeros were an integral part of the livestock export sector; their advance did not represent progress in the manufacturing industry, whose factories and artisan workshops underwent only marginal improvement.

Production was limited by the size of the market, and any extraordinary demand was a welcome bonus. The military policy of Rosas, therefore, had the unqualified support of the industrial sector, for it was war that kept many of these enterprises in business through demands for arms, equipment, hardware, and uniforms. The province had a small armaments industry capable of manufacturing rifles, canons, swords, and gunpowder, though these were also purchased from abroad. Defense expenditure, however, not only stimulated foundries and arms workshops but also gave a boost to other manufactures. The armies of Rosas needed thousands of ponchos, colored jackets, swords, lances, and other equipment in leather, cloth, and metal. War was a lifeline for many workshops in Buenos Aires, and Rosas also used a special military factory in Santos Lugares that employed a large workforce making uniforms and checking weapons. Urban artisans, therefore, were a useful part of the economy. They were numerous enough to carry some weight and, without constituting a major pressure group, to merit consideration. Apart from economic arguments, it was from these groups that Rosas recruited his urban militia. He also seems to have cultivated ethnic minorities as a minor social support. Blacks and mulattos were employed in artisan industries: they manufactured brooms from the shafts of peach trees, clay hearths, leather bags, wicker baskets, and they were in the tailoring, shoe, cigarette, and pastry trades. The presence of blacks in the industrial sector may indeed have been one of the reasons artisans had failed to achieve a high social status and there was always a shortage of skilled labor in spite of relatively high wages.

Outside Buenos Aires there were few industrial activities. In contemporary debate concerning free trade and protection, reference was frequently made to *la industria del país* and *las fábricas de las provincias,* and subsequent historiography has sometimes referred to the industries of the interior as evidence of alternative interests.

But these are difficult to quantify and in some cases to identify. Córdoba had a traditional textile industry that managed to survive in spite of European competition after 1810. Mendoza, producer of wine and brandy in colonial times, succumbed to competition from superior French and Spanish imports. The sub-Andean provinces had mineral resources but not a mining industry; lacking labor and infrastructure, Argentine mining remained a poor investment.

The industries of the interior, therefore, were a minor economic activity. Argentina had a pastoral export economy and a subsistence agriculture. Local industries consisted of a few artisan workshops and some rural domestic production and included processing operations for local products, mainly food and drink. Technology was primitive, the product was frequently inferior and expensive, and outlets were confined to the provincial market. The industries of the interior, in short, were even less advanced than those of Buenos Aires. Woodbine Parish briskly dismissed the possibility of developing a national industry in Argentina with a classic argument when he referred to the dominance of British goods: "As to any native manufactures, it would be idle to think of them in a country as yet so thinly peopled, where every hand is wanted, and may be turned to a tenfold better account, in augmenting its natural resources and means of production, as yet so imperfectly developed."[2]

Economic Nationalism

Argentine industry comprised little more than the artisan goods of Buenos Aires and the processed products of the interior. Yet both these activities came to form an interest and a pressure group, and any regime in Buenos Aires had to define its policy toward them. Rosas believed in the free play of market forces. He maintained that it was necessary to throw off "the prohibitive rules and regulations" imposed by Spain "in times of ignorance and slavery."[3] To achieve economic progress, it was necessary to adopt absolute laissez-faire and thus provide appropriate conditions for the growth of the estancia and the export of its products. Two groups suffered from an indiscriminate application of these policies, the porteño artisans and the provinces. Rosas had inherited a strong position in relation to the provinces, and although he could not determine their internal structures, he was well placed to dictate economic policy because Buenos Aires controlled the river, the port, and the entrance to the interior. Buenos Aires could close the river to any commerce other than its own; it could cut off the Paraná and Uruguay ports from ocean shipping and force the interior provinces to trade through Buenos Aires. Every Argentine product for export and all foreign imports had to pay duties in Buenos Aires. The tariff was not simply a tax, it was an economic policy enabling Buenos Aires to promote certain products in the interior and depress others and at the same time to determine what foreign merchandise the interior should consume. This control could assume political significance, for it gave to porteño governments the means of impoverishing one social group in a province and rewarding another. For all these reasons the most serious challenge to the economic policy of Buenos Aires came from the provinces, and a great debate between free trade and protection was begun.

In July 1830, delegates of Buenos Aires, Santa Fe, Entre Ríos, and Corrientes met in Santa Fe to discuss the terms of what came to be known as the Federal Pact. The leader of the protectionist movement in the littoral was Pedro Ferré, governor of Corrientes, a man descended from a Catalan family though born in the province. He immediately asked Rosas to modify the tariff policies of Buenos Aires in order to protect provincial industry, only to be met with the argument that existing policy had the sanction of Tomás Anchorena, "telling me that for him this man was an oracle and he regarded him as infallible."[4] Ferré posed the question of nationalization of the customs revenue and free navigation of the rivers, arguing that ports other than Buenos Aires should also be authorized to engage directly in foreign trade, thus cutting distances and freightage costs for the interior. These traditional demands of littoral federalism, however, were accompanied by another. Ferré insisted that the provinces be allowed to participate in the control of foreign trade with the object of replacing porteño economic liberalism with a protectionist policy that would promote provincial agriculture and industries by prohibiting the import of products that the country produced. It was not a coincidence that Corrientes took the lead in formulating a protectionist policy; the expansion of its tobacco, cotton, and other subtropical products depended on protection against Paraguayan and, still more, Brazilian competition. Protection was also argued on grounds of job creation, quality of local products, competitive prices, and loss of metallic currency through foreign imports.

José María Rojas y Patrón, the delegate of Buenos Aires, replied that protective duties hit the consumer and did not really help domestic industries if these were not competitive and not capable of supplying the nation's demands. The pastoral economy depended on cheap land, low production costs, and demand for hides in the foreign markets. Protection would raise prices, increase costs, and damage the export trade. Those outside the cattle economy who might conceivably profit from protection were a small minority. The mass of the people depended on foreign trade. He concluded, "Nothing can persuade me that it is right to prohibit certain foreign products in order to promote others which either do not yet exist in this country or are scarce or inferior in quality."[5]

Again Ferré rejected the porteño arguments. In a reply to Rojas, he denounced free competition. Native industries could not compete against cheaper costs of production in foreign countries. So investments were lost, unemployment increased, and the bill for imports was ruinous. The provinces of the littoral and the interior needed protection to save their economies, but Ferré insisted that he sought protection only for those goods the country actually produced, not those it might produce. Provincial federalism was the political expression of economic autonomy; the interior and the littoral sought to defend themselves against the policies of Buenos Aires.

Buenos Aires refused to yield, and the federal treaty of January 4, 1831, was concluded without Corrientes, though it subsequently signed. In a letter to the governor of Catamarca, the Corrientes delegate, Manuel Leyva, accused Buenos Aires of being an obstacle to peace and unity, interested only in retaining national revenues for its own benefit. The letter was intercepted by Facundo Quiroga and forwarded to Rosas, who expressed his outrage. Ferré, however, refused to repudiate the views of Leyva and circulated further arguments to the provincial governors. Buenos Aires, he alleged, was ruining the country's economy, which depended on "the promotion of domestic industry." "If the importation of wines, brandies, textiles and other products furnished by our fertile land were prohibited, production of these would achieve their due importance, and so would all the other branches of national industry."[6] As for foreign trade, this should be encouraged by opening the river ports to overseas shipping.

In Buenos Aires, however, Ferré's circular was denounced: officials pointed to the high costs of production and asked if it was right to tyrannize the great mass of consumers simply for the benefit of the artisans and the farmers. Were there not already duties of 40 percent on foreign wines and spirits and 25 percent on olives? The government invoked other arguments. When, in 1831, Ferré went to Buenos Aires for a meeting with M. J. García, Rosas's finance minister, and pressed on him the need for protecting local agriculture and industry against foreign imports, he was treated to what he called "purely specious" arguments. García maintained that "we are not in a position to take measures against foreign trade, least of all against the English, because we have contracted great debts with that nation and would run the risk of a very damaging rupture. An agreement on protection is a long-term matter; at the moment it has the additional disadvantage that it would diminish the revenues of Buenos Aires and this government would not be able to meet its immense expenditure."[7] Nor could he say when the position would change. Corrientes, however, had its own problems to resolve, as Ferré never ceased to insist. In the period 1825–1830 the province had a negative balance of trade in every year except one.

Economic nationalism was a political force in Buenos Aires as well in the provinces. There was, of course, no such thing as free trade, for the government depended on the customs for the bulk of its income and had to find the correct level of duties to raise revenue without killing off the trade that produced it. Economic attitudes tended to cut across party lines. In general unitarians of the Rivadavia persuasion supported a free-trade position, and federalists stood for a more nationalist policy. But the estancieros were not unqualified protectionists, for they wanted cheap imports, low living and production costs, and good export opportunities. The foreign, and particularly the British, penetration of Buenos Aires, although welcomed by some, was bitterly opposed by others who argued that it signified outside control of trade, competed with local industry, put people out of work, and prevented the growth of a national merchant marine. Not all of these arguments, reiterated then and since, are valid. The British, it is true, introduced after 1810 cheap cotton cloths for popular consumption, but these did not necessarily replace home-produced cloths. To some extent they replaced Peruvian cloths, much in demand in colonial times. More positively they created a completely new demand, for the first time bringing cheap cottons within reach of a mass market. Meanwhile, in the countryside and the interior locally made woolen ponchos coexisted with British textiles at the lower end of the market.[8] Local craft industries in Buenos Aires and the interior, therefore, survived after 1810 even if they underwent a slow and sure decline.

To promote national manufactures, a group of local merchants proposed in 1815 a fiscal policy ranging from high duties to outright prohibition, a strategy seconded by the artisans of Buenos Aires, who throughout the 1820s continued to press for state intervention, demanding the duty-free import of raw materials needed for manufacture and the protection of goods processed out of local products. The estancieros, including Rosas and the Anchorena, preferred free trade to protection in the interests of the export-orientated livestock sector. Consumer interests also opposed protection, for it would restrict supply, remove competitive alternatives, and raise prices.

Free trade was supported by those who opposed state intervention on principle; they argued that industry would flourish only when it was qualified to do so and that national manufactures that could not compete in price and quality with foreign imports were not worth protecting. Pedro de Angelis, one of the more enlightened spokesmen of the Rosas regime, maintained that "before manufacturers we have to be farmers."[9] He strongly attacked the idea of giving protection to the provincial wine industry and the porteño shoe industry on the grounds that protection would raise prices for the mass of consumers and divert to industry labor that would be better employed in the agrarian sector. If there were any hands to spare, they would be more profitably occupied in producing substitutes for imported agricultural products: "Large wheat harvests would be incomparably more useful to the population than all the production of the industries which, at the cost of great sacrifices, we are seeking to promote."[10] Angelis really subscribed to the concept of an international division of labor, against which restrictive laws were either powerless or pernicious.

Nevertheless, concern for the adverse balance of payments, if not for industry and its employees, was sufficient to persuade the government not to close the door to protection. In 1829, imports worth 36,836,601 pesos were offset by exports valued at only 25,561,940 pesos; the country was spending more than it was earning, and the gap had to be filled by the export of specie. The May and June figures for 1832 showed a very unfavorable balance of exports against imports, and again money flowed out of the country. Inflation and the falling value of money eroded what little protection had previously been given. In these circumstances there was a chance for the industrial lobby to be heard. The hat industry and the growing leather-manufacturing industry were among the voices raised demanding protection against the influx of foreign imports, and in some cases against competition for raw materials.

Amid these conflicting views, what were Rosas's intentions? Rivadavia and the unitarians had theoretically supported free trade, though they too depended on customs revenue. Rosas favored the estancieros against farmers and artisans, kept import duties low, and for a long time resisted appeals for intervention. During his first administration there was no significant upward movement in the tariff. A decree of January 7, 1831, imposed a sliding scale on imported flour in the interests of farmers and millers, but the rates were not high enough to be protective, they did not include wheat and other grains, and they did not positively help arable agriculture. In the tariff for 1832 the duty on foreign hats was raised from 9 to 13 pesos per hat in order to protect the domestic industry. During the debate in the House of Representatives some deputies demanded that protection be extended to other domestic industries such as clothes, shoes, and furniture, but the government did not accede, and the special treatment accorded to the hat industry was defended on the grounds that it used local labor and raw materials. The 1835 tariff, passed during the interregnum between the two governments of Rosas, was hotly debated in the House of Representatives. The estancieros made it clear that they wished to maintain a free-trade policy favorable to the export of hides and jerked beef, whereas a "nationalist" minority sought a protective system for local and provincial industries. In the event, the bias against protection remained, and a small revision of the duty on wheat did little to help domestic farmers.

In 1835, anticipating perhaps a new initiative from the incoming government, porteño and provincial demands for protection grew more insistent. So far the tariff policies enacted since Rosas had come to power in 1829 favored the estancieros and saladeristas rather than the province as a whole. He was not prepared to risk higher living

and production costs and thus to damage the export sector; the price
of economic nationalism, he believed, was not worth paying. There
is no evidence that Rosas had an industrial program or a long-term
economic policy for Argentina. But he was not wedded to principle,
and the pragmatist sometimes came to the fore. He was determined
to maintain the dominant structures and interests of the Argentine
economy, but he was also prepared to rescue particular victims of this
economy; thus in due course he heeded the case for protection.

The Customs Law of 1835

In the ley de aduana of December 18, 1835 (for application in
1836), Rosas introduced a significantly higher tariff. From a basic
import duty of 17 percent, the tariff moved upward, giving greater
protection to more vulnerable products until it reached a point of
absolute prohibition. Vital imports such as steel, tin, coal, and agricultural tools were subject to a tax of 5 percent. Sugar, beverages,
and foodstuffs were taxed at 24 percent. A 35 percent tax was
applied to footwear, clothing, furniture, wine, brandy, liquor,
tobacco, oil, and certain leather goods and a tax of 50 percent to
beer, flour, and potatoes. Hats were taxed at 13 pesos each. The
import of a large number of articles was prohibited: these included
textiles and leather products; iron and steel goods and hardware;
wood products; and, when the domestic price fell below 50 pesos a
fanega, wheat. By decree of August 31, 1837, the tariff of 1835 was
amended upward: a surtax of 2 percent was added to imports subject to 10 and 17 percent and a surtax of 4 percent to those subject
to 24 percent. Although the addition was designed to raise revenue
for the Bolivian war, it was continued beyond the conflict and in
effect strengthened the protectionist element. The 1837 measure
was the final increase.

The tariff act of December 1835 was a revision rather than a
reversal of traditional policy. Since 1810 successive governments had
attempted to meet three claims on their tariff policies—customs revenue, free-trade principles, and protection to industry—and to keep
them in correct proportion. The policy of 1835 was new in that it
reduced the bias toward free trade and sought to give positive assistance to the manufacturing industries and arable agriculture; in so

doing, it advanced further toward meeting the demands of the protectionist lobby, to the point of prohibiting the entry of a large number of articles. How did Argentina's chief trading partner react? The British consul thought that the customs law of 1835 would stimulate local industry and agriculture, and the British government did not object to the new tariff scales. The 1837 increases were regarded as more serious, and Lord Palmerston advised the British consul to lecture the government of Buenos Aires on the benefits of free trade.[11] Even so, the British consul was more concerned with consumer purchasing power than with either the tariff or the French blockade; and the fall in demand for "superior" British goods he attributed to the increasing poverty of the middle and lower classes—a consequence of the Bolivian war, conscription, the poor pay of the military, and forced loans. Although the British reacted calmly to the customs law of 1835 and although there were precedents for some of its contents, the fact remains that it was an innovation, a shift toward protection, a concession to national industry and agriculture.

Why did Rosas do it? Did he really believe that Argentina could become more self-sufficient in industry? Was he convinced that the country could decrease its dependence on imports, resist foreign competition, and tolerate higher living costs? Or was he moved by concern for what one historian has called "the welfare of the middle classes," which it would have been politically dangerous to resist?[12] According to this interpretation, the federalist party was losing ground in the mid-1830s and needed to widen its social base by abandoning free trade. Yet the political explanation leads only to further questions. The regime already had a solid base in the estancia. What political difference could a weak industrial sector make? What evidence is there that Rosas needed the support of a minority interest? And even if there were a middle class in Buenos Aires, would all of its members benefit from Rosas's customs law? An alternative explanation uses an argument from nationalism, positing the protective tariff as an attempt to give reality to the Argentine Confederation, planned in the Pact of 1831: Rosas, until then a man of Buenos Aires, began to act as a national ruler in favor of the popular classes and against foreign interests. But a national policy would be expected to include concessions on river navigation and control of customs revenue, and there were no signs that Rosas was thinking in these directions. As for the popular classes, they did not enter his calculation as part of the political nation.

The law itself lacked an explanatory text, but the speech of the governor to the House of Representatives in December 1835 gave some indication of his motives.

> Agriculture and the growing manufacturing industry of the country have long suffered from the absence of protection. And the middle class of our country, unable for lack of capital to participate in the livestock industry, have been deprived of that incentive to work which is normally stimulated by concern to provide for the future of one's children. The government has taken this fact into consideration, noting that foreign agriculture and industry thwart these legitimate aspirations without however bringing noticeable improvement in make or quality.[13]

In other words, without compromising the hegemony of the estancieros, Rosas sought to safeguard the welfare of less privileged sectors; while maintaining the existing economy, he took steps to help its victims.

The ley de aduana of December 1835 cannot be judged exclusively in terms of porteño populism, for it was not based exclusively in social motives. As Rosas himself explained, the law had a strong inter-provincial content: it was designed, if not to promote a national policy, at least to make the federalist policy more credible by giving protection to the provinces as well as to Buenos Aires, and it was an invitation to the provinces to adopt a more collaborative policy in their own customs tariffs. But not all the provinces were reassured, for an unstated assumption of the law of 1835 was that Buenos Aires still controlled the customs and still exercised hegemony over the economic policy of the confederation. Consequently, Rosas had to justify his position and in particular to explain why the *yerba mate* and tobacco of Corrientes were subject to the same duties in Buenos Aires as those from Paraguay and why there was a 20 percent import duty on cigars, again to the detriment of the Corrientes product. He wrote to the governor of Corrientes that to discriminate between the *correntino* and Paraguayan trades would invite contraband: "As for the question of cigars, I had in mind the powerful consideration that in this province there are many poor women who live from this type of industry."[14] There were compensating factors in other parts of the tariff that favored the provinces against Buenos

Aires; an example was the prohibition of the import of foreign ponchos, which were notoriously cheaper to the porteño consumer than the more expensive article (by 30–40 percent) manufactured in the provinces.

Subsequently, after the tariff had been amended upward, Rosas explained in his speech of 1837: "The changes made in the customs law in favor of agriculture and industry have begun to have a good effect. . . . The artisan workshops have employment for young people, who under the vigilance of the police have ceased to disturb the streets and thoroughfares, and one should hope that the prosperity of these classes will increase the import of the numerous articles of foreign industry which have not been prohibited or charged with extra duties. In fact foreign trade grows perceptibly." Finally, he again explained that the customs law was "not an act of egoism" and that Buenos Aires expected the provinces to reciprocate by not putting up barriers against her trade. The inconsistencies in these statements may be explained by the fact that Rosas genuinely sought something for everyone, above all for estancieros and saladeristas but also for merchants, artisans, workers, and farmers. He went on to claim that the restoration of law and order had benefited everyone, including the poor: "Everyone is rich even in his poverty, since he knows that what he has is his own and whatever he earns he can possess."[15] This was a complacent view, no doubt, but a characteristic one. In these words, Rosas bestowed his blessing on the existing order of society, not on change.

High Tariffs, Low Expectations

The effects of the protective tariff of 1835 were far from clear. The first to benefit were apparently the farmers. Grain prices improved, to the satisfaction of growers in Buenos Aires province and the interior; there was some diversification and a steady increase in the production of wheat, maize, and vegetables up to 1850 and beyond. In 1835–1838 there was even an export of wheat, flour, and maize. Farming continued to lack stable conditions, however, and grain prices oscillated. In some years high prices were a stimulus; in others, they were so high as to indicate want of supply. Blockades gave agriculture added protection, but then consumers experienced severe shortages. In the late 1840s, North American flour was still imported. In good years such as 1850, the flour producers of Buenos Aires could supply the home market and still have a surplus for export, but arable agriculture was now beset by another challenge for land, from the growing sheep sector. Meanwhile, the wine and brandy producers of the interior, unable or unwilling to improve their product, did not emerge from depression in spite of protection.

The response of local industries to protection was slow and feeble. Some critics were quick to claim that the tariffs were too low. The shoemakers of Buenos Aires, one of the biggest groups of artisans, alleged in 1836 that a 35 percent import duty did not give adequate protection and that only a total ban on imported footwear would halt the mounting loss of capital, short workdays, closures, and unemployment. The complaints were probably exaggerated: although there was certainly keen foreign competition at the upper end of the market, there was only limited importation of shoes, and Buenos Aires normally exported locally made footwear to other provinces. Arguments from the industrial sector, therefore, did not necessarily impress the government. In any case, there were soon other pressures on its economic policy.

The first French blockade (1838–1840) caused severe shortages in Buenos Aires, in effect providing a surfeit of protection. By the decree of May 28, Rosas reduced duties on all imports by one-third in order to induce foreigners to break the blockade and sustain supplies. After the blockade, Rosas decided to allow the entry of all goods previously prohibited in order to relieve scarcity; these included iron and tin manufactures, vehicle wheels, and some textiles. This departure from the law of 1835 suggests that either protection or the blockade or a combination of the two had reduced imports but that local industry could not make up for the consequent shortages. The decree was the end of import prohibition. In 1845, when Buenos Aires was blockaded for the second time, by Britain as well as France, Rosas again had to modify the tariff downward, and import duties were reduced by one-third. Imports flowed through the blockade, and domestic products suffered. In 1848 the French blockade was lifted and the tariffs of 1835 were restored; they were little more than a formality, useful only for raising revenue.

What options did Rosas have? The impoverishment of the

province combined with currency depreciation and loss of purchasing power—the paper peso had lost more than half its 1835 gold value by 1850—inhibited industrial development by reducing the market for domestic industry. So the tariff, even when it was effective, merely caused shortages and high prices and raised the cost of living for the mass of the people. Rosas therefore tacitly abandoned the attempt to promote national industries by further tariff protection, and in the last years of his regime, estancieros and consumers were better served, whereas artisans had to be content with existing tariffs. The estancieros had probably suffered less than other sectors from the blockades, for they could stockpile and multiply their cattle herds while waiting for the reopening of foreign trade. Then, once the blockade was lifted, there was a spurt of demand for foreign consumer goods. The British did not appear to be unduly troubled by tariffs or blockades. When Charles Mansfield visited the River Plate in 1852–1853, he traveled like a walking advertisement for British goods: his white cotton poncho, bought in Corrientes, was made in Manchester; his electroplated spurs, bought in Buenos Aires, were made in Birmingham.

How, then, did national production respond to protection? It was incapable of exploiting the opportunity. A single law, of course, could not in itself effect structural change or reallocate resources within the economy. A tariff policy alone could not give local industry the infrastructure needed for development, and its effectiveness was offset by other factors. The cost of freightage from the interior in a country of vast distances and primitive transport was still extremely high. Thus, the goods from the provinces were encumbered with heavy transport costs before they even met the competition of international prices in the littoral. Protection meant giving artificial respiration to the weakest sector of the economy while strangling the stronger. Few people would thank a government for that. Rosas himself appears to have lost faith in protection, though he did not formally abandon it. The industrial sector was not important or large enough to constitute a power base, and there was no necessity for Rosas either to appease it or to cultivate it. If he did so, temporarily, he seems to have been pursuing a preferred social policy to assist those left behind by the prevailing economy and to take account of exceptions to the general rule, the hegemony of the estancia. An alternative Argentina did not exist and could not yet emerge.

5

LEVIATHAN

The Rosas System

Rosas divided society into those who commanded and those who obeyed. Order obsessed him, and the virtue that he most admired in a people was obedience. His view of Argentine history reflected these simple ideas. The Revolution of May 1810 he saw as a necessary evil; it gave Argentina independence, but it left a vacuum in which disorder prevailed and violence ruled. He himself came forward to rescue the country from chaos in 1829; then, at last, it was seen that theory was an illusion, democracy utopia, and liberty a form of slavery. The estanciero who had given detailed instructions to his overseers and staked out his peons in the sun became the governor who goaded his justices of the peace and filled the gaols to overflowing. In place of a constitution, he demanded total sovereignty, and in 1835, he justified the possession of "a power without limits" as vital to dispel anarchy: "I have been careful not to make any other use of it than is absolutely necessary for the order and peace of the country."[1] Later, in Southampton, he claimed that he had taken over an anarchic, divided, disintegrating, bankrupt, and unstable country, "a hell in miniature," and made it a place fit to live in. "For me the ideal of good government would be paternal autocracy, intelligent, disinterested and indefatigable. . . . I have always admired the autocratic dictators who have been the first servants of their people."[2] But what Rosas saw as a benevolent despotism, other Argentines regarded as a ruthless tyranny.

If there was anything more abhorrent to Rosas than democracy, it was liberalism. He detested unitarians not because they wanted a united Argentina but because they were liberals who believed in the

75

secular values of humanism and progress. He identified them with freemasons and intellectuals, men of enlightenment and principles, subversives who undermined order and tradition and whom he held ultimately responsible for the political assassinations that brutalized Argentine public life from 1828 to 1835. The constitutional doctrines of unitarians and federalists did not interest him, and he was never a true federalist. In 1829, he denied belonging to the federal or to any party and expressed contempt for Dorrego. He thought and ruled as a centralist and stood for the hegemony of Buenos Aires. He explained political divisions in terms of social structure. He interpreted the conflict of 1828–1829 and its aftermath as a war between the poorer classes and the mercantile aristocracy. "The question is between an aristocratic minority and a republican majority." "The federal masses are composed of the people of the countryside and the lower orders of the city, but these are not the people who direct the policy of the government."[3] And on occasion he explained his federalism faute de mieux: "I am convinced that Federation is the form of government which most conforms to the democratic principles in which we were educated in the colonial period, when the ranks and titles of aristocracy were unknown here, unlike Chile and Lima. . . . Nevertheless, although I am Federal by conviction I would undertake to be a Unitarian if the vote of the peoples were for Unity."[4] Unity, he used to say, was more appropriate to an aristocracy, federalism to a democracy. In April 1839, he preached to his coterie in the evening under the ombu trees at Palermo, as reported by his secretary, the conspirator Enrique Lafuente: "He argued that we were democrats or federals, which for him is the same, since the time of the Spaniards."[5]

But this statement was political rhetoric. There was no democracy in Argentina, and the people did not rule. This is not to deny that there was some positive response to Rosas. Support among porteños for the dictator reflected the personal benefits, especially the improved chances in life, derived from his imposed domestic peace. In this sense the dictatorship derived its legitimacy from the protection and benefit accorded to the mass of the people.[6]

Rosas was a skillful manipulator. He manipulated the lower sectors, as has been seen, but he did not represent them and did not enfranchise them. He had a horror of social revolution, and he cultivated the popular classes not to give them power or property but to divert them from insubordination and violence. He believed he had a lesson to teach other rulers. The Revolution of 1848 in France drew his strong disapproval. He saw it as a conflict between those who had no stake in society and sensible men of property; the French government was itself to blame for not paying attention to the lower classes. What he advocated, of course, was not social reform but propaganda and constraint. Rosas himself had an instinct for manipulating the discontents of the masses and turning them against his enemies in such a way that they not damage the basic structure of society. By a mixture of demagogy and nationalism, he was able skillfully to give an illusion of popular participation and a community of interest between patrón and peon. But his federalism had little social content. In fact, Rosas destroyed the traditional division between federalists and unitarians and made these categories virtually meaningless. He substituted rosismo and antirosismo.

What was rosismo? Its power base was the estancia, a focus of economic resources and a system of social control. The estancia gave Rosas the sinews of war, the alliance of fellow estancieros, and the means of recruiting an army of peons, gauchos, and vagrants. In 1829, he not only defeated his unitarian enemies, he also demonstrated his ability to control popular forces. He then so exploited men's fear of anarchy that he was able to demand and obtain absolute power. Thus armed, he proceeded to take total possession of the state apparatus—the bureaucracy, the police, the standing army. With the ultimate means of coercion in his hands, he ceased to rely on the irregular forces of the countryside. They could return home, as it were—the estancieros to cultivate their estates, the gauchos to become ranch hands or to serve in the regular army. Rosas now exercised a monopoly of power in a state geared to the interests of the estancieros and a primitive export economy. As populism receded, persuasion took its place; control, coercion, and propaganda became intrinsic to the regime. Total political control was imposed. In this sense, rosismo was a classical despotism, but it was despotism with a novel organization and with its own style. No rival loyalties were allowed, no alternative parties permitted. The populace was relentlessly indoctrinated by a regime that controlled all the means of communication. Rosas was built into a great leader figure, a one-man government, a protector and father of his people, and a single political movement took the place of constitutional choice.

Party activists in alliance with the police applied systematic terrorism against the enemy within. The detection of dissidents and the destruction of opponents engaged a large part of the resources of the state as a system of conformity was applied that was almost totalitarian in character. Pacification had its price.

This regime gave Rosas hegemony in Buenos Aires for over twenty years. But he could not apply the same strategy to the whole of Argentina. In the provinces of the west, Rosas was seen as a caudillo who served the local interests of Buenos Aires; there the loyalty of the hacendados and the service of their peons were not so easily procured. In the interior the federal party had weaker economic roots and a narrower social base; and in the remoter parts of the confederation, it could not immediately apply autocratic domination or regulate the use of terror. The pacification of the interior, therefore, meant the conquest of the interior by Buenos Aires. Federalism gave way to rosismo. This solution, however, could not be applied to the littoral provinces, where foreign intervention in alliance with local dissent prevented the total hegemony of Buenos Aires and ultimately tipped the balance against Rosas.

Limitless Power

The advent of Rosas to power in 1829 was regarded as a restoration after the interregnum of the usurper Lavalle. The House of Representatives approved retrospectively all his political and military conduct as commander general of the countryside from December 1, 1828, to December 8, 1829, when he became governor of Buenos Aires endowed with extraordinary powers; declared him Restorer of the Laws and Institutions of the Province of Buenos Aires; and plied him with other titles and decorations. There was, of course, no ideological cohesion in the country, no social unity behind accepted values. So the restoration appealed to interests rather than to ideas. Rosas represented powerful interest groups, estancieros and businessmen, who wanted peace and security and who equated the unitarian governments of Rivadavia and Lavalle with innovation and instability. The first government of Rosas (1829–1832) subordinated everything to law and order. He strengthened the army and protected the church; he silenced critics and ignored education. He did not ignore the poor, or at least those who had impoverished themselves in the federal cause during the war of 1828–1829 by supplying goods and services to Rosas's forces; these he compensated, or promised to compensate, out of public funds. But he took revenge on his unitarian enemies and effectively muzzled the press, which now became a mere mouthpiece of the government.

Rosas ruled from 1829 to 1832 with absolute sovereignty. Faced by some opposition in the assembly, he demanded a reform of the constitution to extend the extraordinary powers of the government. When this demand was rejected he refused to accept reelection as governor and ended his term of office on December 5, 1832. After an interregnum, during which he commanded the Desert Campaign and strengthened his power base in the countryside while his supporters destabilized the government in Buenos Aires, he returned to power in dramatic circumstances. Facundo Quiroga, the veteran caudillo of the interior and scourge of the unitarians, was chosen by Buenos Aires to lead a mission of pacification to the northwest. Returning from his mission, he was ambushed and assassinated by his political enemies at Barranca Yaco on February 16, 1835. The death of Quiroga eased the ascent of Buenos Aires in the confederation. It also prepared the way for the return of Rosas to power. For these reasons, it was rumored that Rosas himself was responsible for the assassination, but if Rosas was the beneficiary of the crime, there is no evidence to indicate that he was the author.

As soon as the news of Quiroga's assassination was officially announced to the House of Representatives the deputies fell over each other to rise and call on Rosas to save the country from anarchy, as he had done once before. If necessary, he must be given absolute power to rescue the country from destruction and to satisfy his own demands. Rosas kept them waiting. At length, on March 16, 1835, he addressed the House, expressing his thanks for the offer of extraordinary powers and lamenting the imminent danger that threatened the country from the divisions of opinion, the clash of interests, and the pretensions of individuals, all of which had totally paralyzed the action of the executive. The only way of resolving the problem was to give him the entire sum of public power, but with the backing of public opinion, "that each and every one of the inhabitants of the city, of all classes and conditions, may register their votes precisely and categorically upon the matter."[7]

The plebiscite was held on March 26–28 in the parishes of Buenos Aires city, and the electorate had to vote yes or no for the projected law: this vote was not exactly to elect him but to "express their opinion" on his election. Voters comprised "every free man, native of the country, or residing in it, from the age of twenty years."[8] Universal male suffrage was not new in Argentina. It had been first established in 1821. This time there were two differences. First, the plebiscite was held only in Buenos Aires city, presumably to save time and on the assumption that the countryside was completely rosista. Second, whereas normally only a few hundred people voted at elections, this time greater numbers participated. The result was 9,316 for the new law, 4 against. If we assume a population of some 60,000 in Buenos Aires and a voting population of 20,000, Rosas received a vote of 50 percent of the electorate, and even this portion was urged to the polls by a mixture of official propaganda and pressure from activists. The menace exerted by Rosas's political machine was real enough, as shall be seen. For this reason the heavy abstentions were significant; to abstain was a positive and dangerous act, and for many people a militant one. Rosas never repeated the experiment.

Following the referendum, the majority of the deputies supported the new law, and it was finally sanctioned on April 1, 1835, giving Rosas unlimited power for a term of five years. His inauguration was accompanied by a proliferation of parades and ceremonies and a frenzy of adulation as the various social groups, the military, merchants, officials, and others competed to show their loyalty to Rosas. Adulation became idolatry as portraits of the Restorer were placed on the altars of the principal churches. Rosas's particular contribution to these celebrations was a proclamation promising to use his limitless power to bring swift judgment and death to the regime's enemies, "so that not one of this race of monsters may remain among us" and in the hope that others would be frightened off.[9] He saw himself as a dictator by divine right and regarded the retribution he delivered as an act of God.

The demonstrations were officially inspired, and as an outward sign of inward submission, they anticipated the Rosas style of government: passive obedience was not enough; Rosas wanted absolute and

active support from every institution in the land, from the House of
Representatives, the law courts, the bureaucracy, the press, the church,
and the military—from patrón and from peon. As Rosas controlled all
the institutions of state and society, there was no toleration of opposition and no opportunity for dissent, only a clandestine and dangerous existence. Rosas proclaimed a sole and exclusive truth in politics.

Total Government

The House of Representatives remained a creature of the governor,
whom it formally "elected." It was his custom to send his resignation to the House from time to time. It was never accepted, for the
House of Representatives represented only the regime. It consisted
of forty-four deputies, half of whom were annually renewed by election. But only a small minority of the electorate participated, and it
was the duty of the justices of the peace to deliver these votes to the
government. The assembly, lacking for the most part legislative
function and financial control, was largely an exercise in public relations for the benefit of foreign and domestic audiences, and it normally responded obsequiously to the initiatives of the governor.

Rosas not only controlled the legislature but also dominated the
judicial power. He not only made law; he interpreted it, changed it,
and applied it. The machinery of justice no doubt continued to function: the justices of the peace, judges for civil and criminal cases, the
appeal judge, and the supreme court all gave institutional legitimacy
to the regime. But the law did not rule. Arbitrary intervention by the
executive undermined the independence of the judiciary. Rosas took
many cases on himself, read the evidence (often supplied by his local
henchman Vicente González), examined the police reports, and, as
he sat alone at his desk, gave judgment, writing on the files "shoot
him," "fine him," "imprison him," "to the army."

Rosas justified the executive's usurpation of the role of the judiciary in terms of the extraordinary powers: "Even though I have
been invested by the House of Representatives with the *suma del
poder público,* I am very conscious of the object for which this high
and extraordinary power was granted. So I have taken care to make
no other use of it than is essential for the general order and peace of
the country, as far as possible leaving all cases to the due process of

law, as long as this is not in opposition to political objectives." In short, Rosas was an absolute ruler. "As he told me himself," remarked the British minister Southern, "he wields a power more absolute than any monarch on his throne."[10]

Rosas also controlled the bureaucracy. One of his first and most uncompromising measures was to purge the old administration; this action was the simplest way of removing political enemies and rewarding followers, and it was inherent in the patrón-client organization of society. He himself expressed the move in loftier terms. After a period of extreme political violence, he explained to the provinces, the only method of government remaining was that of "purging everything not in conformity with the general will of the Republic. Nothing doubtful, nothing false, nothing suspect ought to exist in the Federal cause."[11] The entire policy of *depuración* was designed to eliminate the enemy within; the victims were alleged unitarians or simply people who were not sufficiently ardent in their federalism. The beneficiaries were part of the clientela whom the caudillo had accumulated on his way to power, many of them belonging to the Rosas family network. The new administration was not extravagantly large, and further economy was imposed by leaving vacancies unfilled. Appointments of all kinds were reserved for political clients and federalists; other qualifications counted for little. Rosas instinctively distrusted reformed unitarians and converted federalists and refused to have them in his administration, arguing that they regarded amnesty as a sign of weakness: "They will learn to improve and co-operate with us when they see that we are resolute in punishing the wicked and rewarding the good." In short, Rosas was a dictator, the name employed by exiles such as Sarmiento and Alberdi.

The system of government Rosas and his colleagues operated was primitive in the extreme and completely lacked a constitutional framework. They did not govern Argentina. The thirteen provinces governed themselves independently, though they were grouped in the general Confederation of the United Provinces of the Río de la Plata. Even without formal union, however, the provinces were forced to delegate certain common interests to the government of Buenos Aires, mainly defense and foreign policy and occasionally an element of legal jurisdiction; when Rosas claimed the judgment and execution of Quiroga's assassins for Buenos Aires, he persuaded the provinces to agree in effect that theirs was a federal crime. Rosas, therefore, exercised some de facto control over the provinces, partly to prevent subversion and anarchy seeping into Buenos Aires, partly to have a secure base for economic and foreign policy, and partly to acquire a national dimension for his regime. His policy was to wear down the provincial caudillos, to conquer them by patience. In each of the provinces, he managed gradually to impose allied, satellite, or weak governors.

In interprovincial relations, Rosas preferred informal power to a written constitution. He always refused to prepare a constitution, arguing that the provinces would have to organize themselves before the time would be opportune for national organization; the progress of the parts must precede that of the whole, and the first task was to defeat the unitarians. As he advised Quiroga before his last mission, "Without well-organized states, capable of governing themselves and ensuring due order, the federal republic is chimerical and would be disastrous."[12]

The Cult of Rosas

Propaganda was an essential element of rosismo: a few simple and barbarous slogans passed for ideology, and these permeated the administration and impressed a nervous public. The language of politics was charged with violence and designed to terrorize. People were obliged to dress in a kind of uniform and to use the federalist color, red. Women were expected to wear red ribbons in their hair, men to have a fierce and hirsute look and wear red silk badges bearing the inscription "Long live the Argentine Confederation. Death to the Savage Unitarians." This was also the heading of official documents. One senior official who forgot to head a decree with the federal slogan groveled before Rosas to beg his forgiveness, his servility exceeded only by his fear: "I swear by all that is sacred that my failure to write the words 'savage unitarian' could only have been an unintentional mistake. . . . It is inconceivable that I should have decided deliberately to omit the words 'savage unitarian,' which I believe are not only accurate but deserved."[13] The symbolism was a form of coercion and conformity. To adopt the federal look and the federal language took the place of security checks and oaths of allegiance. Federal uniformity was a measure of totalitarian pressure by which people were forced to stop thinking for themselves, to abandon a passive or apolitical role and to accept a specific commitment, to show their true colors. Political ritual of this kind was unique in Spanish America and anticipated the style of later dictatorships. An invention of Rosas himself, it was an object of contempt among his more cultivated followers but adopted with enthusiasm by his coarser retinue.

The church was a willing ally, and no occasion was missed to identify federalism with religion. The higher clergy were solidly behind Rosas, urging the faithful to give total support to the restorer of the laws and the defender of religion. Bishop Mariano Medrano of Buenos Aires, who wore federal vestments with elaborate emblems, instructed the priests of the diocese to preach to women and young people the virtue of belonging to the federal cause. Most of the lower clergy were vehemently pro-Rosas; they were virtually another arm of his populism, minor caudillos of the regime, often violently disposed toward unitarians, whom they blamed for the anticlerical measures of Rivadavia and on whom they now called for vengeance. The church in turn received the support of Rosas, at a price.

Rosas was a conventional Catholic from birth and upbringing. He prayed, believed in Divine Providence, and regarded unitarians as enemies of Jesus Christ. He promptly ended the liberalism and anticlericalism of Rivadavia, restored churches, reinstated the Dominicans, and authorized the return of the Jesuits. But he had a utilitarian conception of religion and valued it above all as a support of social order and subordination. Although he protected the church, he also dominated and manipulated it, treating the clergy as a branch of the bureaucracy and expecting it to serve the federal cause in all things. He claimed the right of patronage, used it to appoint only federalists in the church, and kept papal jurisdiction out of Argentina. By decree of February 27, 1837, he declared null any papal bull introduced since 1810 and any ecclesiastical appointment contained therein. And as late as 1851, he refused to negotiate with a papal envoy who had been sent to resolve the patronage dispute.

The Jesuits returned to Argentina in 1836, about seventy years after their expulsion by Charles III. They came at the invitation of Rosas, who restored them to their former church and college of San Ignacio and allowed them to open schools, to plan missions to the

Indians, and to settle in Córdoba as well as Buenos Aires. But they proved a disappointment to the caudillo. They actually remained aloof from federal politics, refused to allow their schools and churches to become centers of federal propaganda, and resisted attempts to co-opt them into the regime. Soon they were harassed by activists and terrorized by the mazorca, and in 1843–1844 Rosas expelled them, allegedly for seeking domination and power and for accepting rule from Rome. The Jesuits became a test of the totalitarian tendency of the regime. It was impossible to be neutral in the struggle between the official truth and its enemies; one was either pro-Rosas or anti-Rosas. The dictator expected the Jesuits to accept from the government "the rules, principles and political system in which they must instruct our youth."[14] He planned to make them ideological agents of the regime. In the event, he proved what his enemies had long alleged, that not the slightest degree of deviation, not the smallest amount of independence, not a single enclave, was tolerated in the Argentina of Rosas.

Political orthodoxy was conveyed by word as well as by deed, and the printing presses of Buenos Aires—five in all—were kept fully employed turning out newspapers in Spanish and other languages with official news and propaganda for circulation at home and abroad. The *Gaceta Mercantil* also expressed, however incoherently, the political ideas of Rosas, his "Americanism" and his efforts to inculcate a sense, if not of Argentine nationalism, at least of independent identity. As Southern observed:

> He evidently regrets the absence in these people of a spirit of national independence: with a view of exciting this feeling—a powerful instrument in the hands of an efficient ruler—many of the documents and speeches in the Gazette are expressly written and published. The "Gazeta Mercantil" which is immediately under his care . . . is read every day in every corner of the country by the district authorities; the judge of peace reads it to the civilians, and the military commandant to the persons connected with the Army. The Gazette is in fact part of a simulacrum of government, which is kept up with a perfection of which only a man of the force of character, and of the inflexible and untiring nature of general Rosas is capable.[15]

Rosas came to have his principal residence at Palermo, some four miles from the city center, where a staff of 300 ranging from officials and secretaries to servants, overseers, and peons served the caudillo.

More than one English visitor remarked on his country style, his ruddy countenance and stout figure: "In appearance Rosas resembles an English gentleman farmer—his manners are courteous without being refined. He is affable and agreeable in conversation, which however nearly always turns on himself, but his tone is pleasant and agreeable enough. His memory is stupendous: and his accuracy in all points of detail never failing."[16] One of his secretariat reported: "This tiger is very tame towards his immediate servants";[17] but he was a hard taskmaster and could suddenly fly into a rage and emit threats of throat cutting like the vilest of his henchmen. Surrounded by his staff, Rosas placed himself at a distance from his ministers; in effect, he reduced the system of government to two sectors: his personal secretariat, which exercised real power, and the ministries, whose function was more formal. This was personal government of the crudest kind; all policy decisions and most executive ones were made by Rosas, often dictated while striding up and down his long office, his secretaries scurrying after him. No attempt was made to organize the delegation of administrative powers and functions. The only exception was the work done by his daughter, Manuelita, who acted as a kind of filter through whom business of an extrajudicial character, including petitions for clemency, was transmitted.

Government by Force

Whereas the church and the press were essential auxiliaries of the Rosas government, the ultimate sanction was force, applied by the military and the police and financed from the meager income enjoyed by the state. The regime was not, strictly speaking, a military dictatorship; it was a civilian regime that employed a compliant military. The military establishment, however, existed not only to defend the country but also to occupy it, not only to protect the population but also to control it. On the Chacarita road about ten miles west of Buenos Aires and alongside a miserable Indian settlement lay Santos Lugares de Morón, military headquarters, army camp, and political prison. This was the principal pillar of the regime, erected by Rosas in the late 1830s. Its established strength was about 5,000, divided into three divisions: infantry, cavalry, and artillery. The barracks consisted of rows of primitive huts built by the soldiers themselves, a few officers' quarters, and a pulpería. The military forces were composed of the regular army and the militia. But the distinction between military and civilians in a country where estancieros could lead into action squadrons of mounted peons was not absolute, and the paramilitary capability of the estancieros acted as a constraint on the power of the professional military.

The Law of Militia of December 17, 1823, established in the province of Buenos Aires the infantry militia, divided into active-service units (members aged 17–45) and reservists (aged 45–65), and the cavalry, consisting of active-service units only (members aged 20–45). The active-service militia had a strength of eleven battalions in the capital and thirteen in the country; it was recruited and controlled by the commanders general of militias and the justices of the peace, often the same people; its role was to supplement the regular army. This was the militia organization that Rosas inherited and did so much to improve. He employed it to keep law and order, to suppress rebellion, to fortify the federal regime in the countryside, and in practice to replenish the ranks of the regular army. Essentially the militia consisted of estancieros leading their peons; there was indeed a special elitist corps, the Guardía de Honor del Restaurador, formed by leading hacendados.

The hierarchy of the land was built into the militia, where the estancieros were the commanders, the overseers were the officers, and the peons were the troops. From top to bottom there was firm control based on a patrón-client relationship. Rosas also had an urban militia, recruited mainly from artisans, retail traders, and shopkeepers. Some of these were also members of the mazorca, though the leadership of this semiofficial terrorist organization came from ex-militia officers and other members of the higher sectors. There was also a force of blacks and mulattos, the so-called negrada federal, black troops in red uniforms. These urban militias were not very impressive militarily, though the blacks looked fearsome enough; but they were a social force for Rosas, and he seems to have cultivated the coloreds in particular.

The military power of the Rosas regime, however, rested not only on militias and montoneros but also on a regular army officered by professional soldiers. Senior officers such as Prudencio Rosas and Lucio Mansilla were part of the family network of the dictator; others, such as Angel Pacheco and Juan Isidro Quesada, were closely committed to the regime. The prototype was Angel Pacheco, a very model of the rosista general. Physically tough and erect with a severe expression and smart uniform, Pacheco was a professional soldier to the core, a cruel fighter who had earned his experience on the battlefield in the wars of independence, the Indian frontier, and the civil wars. His political views were simple: he hated all unitarians, whom he regarded as the ruin of the country and the allies of the national enemy, the French. With generals like Pacheco, Rosas had no problems with his higher command. This loyalty was important, for lower down the line, military virtues were less obvious.

The army of Rosas was an army of conscripts. As the rural population was unwilling to serve and landowners reluctant to lose their labor supply, *levas* were raised by law and imposed by force; conscripts were rounded up by military patrols, which in effect were press-gangs and herded men from the estates or hunted them down in open country. The first victims of the levies, therefore, were law-abiding men who offered no resistance. Further targets were delinquents, and delinquency was so defined as to include vagrants and the nonemployed as well as criminals and outlaws. Many of the troops were blacks and mulattos, some of them slaves who earned their freedom through enlistment. The demagogic relationship of Rosas with the lower sectors could not disguise his fundamental disdain for them, and if he showed any favor to coloreds, it was within the existing structure.

The army of Rosas, therefore, was not a popular army. It was an incoherent, apolitical multitude of more or less reluctant conscripts, for many of whom military life was a form of imprisonment, and it was led by professional officers of varying degrees of experience. Military service, however, was a burden not only on the common people of the countryside but also on the estancieros, or at least on those without influence in the administration, for it aggravated the labor shortage by forcefully taking away vital employees of the estancia, not to mention valuable broken-in horses. One way to avoid this conscription was by special privilege, such as the Anchorenas enjoyed. The only other way was to pay for substitutes, which was a form of taxation. Otherwise estancieros and peons were at the mercy of local military commanders who spared their friends and exacted unfair levies on others. The burden grew intolerable in the 1840s, after a decade of provincial and foreign wars, and as arbitrary and ruthless exactions grew so did the protests.

Forces of this kind had low morale, and little sense of duty or patriotism; national spirit and motivation were virtually nonexistent except among officers, whose role was not only to lead their troops but also to retain them. Desertion was endemic, and deserters became a new plague on the pampas, a further quarry for patrols. The reward was twenty pesos for a deserter, who could be shot if caught. In this respect there was little difference between the federal and the unitarian armies: neither were popular forces, and both were decimated by desertions. The authorities tried various means of keeping an army together. Camp followers, called Chinas, were a recognized part of the organization; mounted like their menfolk, they not only followed but sometimes fought. "Through all these provinces it is customary for every soldier, during a campaign, to be allowed a woman as a companion, who regularly receives rations. . . . The authorities allege that such license is absolutely necessary to the well-being of the army; the men being less disposed to desert when they have a female companion, who attends to the working, cooking, and needlework."[18]

Armies were also kept together by hope of reward. Booty was an accepted means of financing and sustaining an army, whether it was federal or unitarian. In default of adequate revenue and in conditions of scarce resources, the war effort was supported by raids on estancias for horses and supplies or by the despoliation of those parts of the country that did not support the federal cause. Authorized robbery was virtually the only prize available for the common soldier when his wages were overdue. Thus, pillage became institutionalized, and armies lived off the land. Officers also received land grants, and in the case of generals and colonels, these amounted to vast estates carved out of new land on the Indian frontier, public land, and confiscations. Land grants of this kind were made periodically after the Desert Campaign, the rebellion of the south, and other important operations with the land units always carefully graded according to rank. Few common soldiers could aspire to such prizes. Theoretically they too shared in the land awards, but in practice it was difficult, if not impossible, for them to claim their grants or to exploit them; normally they had to be satisfied with a uniform, a daily meat ration, and twenty pesos a month. The clientela also had their hierarchy, and it too reflected the social structure.

Maintenance of the military establishment and support for its privileged position in society were a heavy burden on the rest of the population. Moreover, this was an active military constantly engaged in foreign wars, interprovincial conflicts, and internal security. But war and the economic demands of war, whereas they meant misery for the many, made fortunes for the few. Defense spending provided a secure market for certain industries and employment for their workers: the fairly constant demand for uniforms, arms, and equipment helped to sustain a number of artisan manufactures in an otherwise depressed industrial sector. Above all, the military market benefited several large landowners. Proprietors such as the Anchorenas had long and valuable contracts for the supply of cattle to frontier forts. Now the armies on other fronts became voracious consumers and regular customers, generating profits for estancieros.

How large was the army of Rosas? The various divisions covering different fronts were not large individually, but together they amounted to a sizable force. In 1841 the British minister believed they totaled 16,000 men. Another estimate, in 1845, placed the figure at 10,000, and a French observer spoke of an army of 21,600 men. No one doubted that Rosas maintained a large standing army in relation to the level of population.

Priorities

The army and its liabilities increased at a time when revenue was contracting, and something had to give. When the French blockade began to bite, from April 1838, not only were people thrown out of work and hit by rapid inflation but the government saw its revenue from customs—its basic income—fall dramatically. Faced with heavy budget deficits, it immediately imposed severe expenditure cuts: "Some of the public institutions have been suspended, among the latter the public schools and the foundling hospital. An appeal has been made to the public for subscriptions to support the hospitals of men and women, which are to be closed if the amount received be not sufficient for their maintenance."[19]

The army and its suppliers survived intact, but other sectors were less fortunate. Education, social services, and welfare in general were badly crippled as their income from public funds dwindled to a trickle. Although education was by no means extinguished, it suffered from financial starvation as well as indoctrination. Primary schools in Buenos Aires were neglected by the state and attended by only a small percentage of children of school age, and in the countryside, provision for education was even worse. Secondary education consisted of two colleges, one of which had a subvention from the government. Even these modest services were almost completely deprived of funds in April 1838, when a series of decrees stopped state money to schools, colleges, and the university. The latter was virtually closed because professional salaries were suppressed, though alternative arrangements were made for teaching law and medicine. The Sociedad de Beneficencia, which had been founded in 1823 for the care and education of girls, was not actually closed down but received no income after 1838. Meanwhile, nothing was done for the other face of Buenos Aires, the limbo world of urban slums where filthy hovels in a wasteland of mud or dust provided homes for the outcasts of society. As the French observer Xavier Marmier observed, "Rosas has not yet deigned to descend into this miserable half of his capital; he has failed to repair these filthy streets and open drains with any of the funds which the House of Representatives lavish upon him so freely."[20] The House was not so lavish or Rosas so well funded, and when priorities were tested, the dictator did not make even a pretence of governing by popular mandate.

The contrast between military and social spending reflected circumstances as well as values. The enemy within, conflict with other provinces and with foreign powers, and the obligation to succor his allies in the interior all caused Rosas to maintain a heavy defense budget. Some of these choices were forced on him, others were preferred policy, yet others reflected a universal indifference toward welfare. In any case the consequences were social retardation. In the 1840s the ministry of government, or home affairs, received on average between 6 and 7 percent of the total budget, and most of this was allocated to police and political expenditure, not to social services. Defense, in contrast, received absolute priority. The military budget varied from 4 million pesos, or 27 percent of the total, in 1836 to 23.8 million, 49 percent, during the French blockade in

Table 5.1   Distribution of Government Expenditure,
1840–1850 (percentage of total)

Year	War	Govern- ment	Foreign Affairs	Treasury	Long-term Debt	Treasury Bills	House of Represen- tatives
1840	49.1	3.0	2.8	3.5	6.3	35.2	0.1
1841	71.1	5.0	2.4	3.8	9.0	8.7	0.1
1842	63.4	4.8	1.8	6.8	10.3	12.8	0.1
1843	53.1	6.1	2.3	9.1	10.7	18.6	0.1
1844	61.0	7.2	2.3	7.9	10.9	10.7	0.1
1845	54.7	6.2	3.8	8.5	11.1	15.6	0.1
1846	49.5	7.0	5.8	6.2	12.0	19.4	0.1
1847	57.9	7.2	4.5	5.4	9.6	15.2	0.1
1848	55.7	6.6	4.7	5.9	10.0	17.1	0.1
1849	58.3	8.4	3.3	4.7	7.8	17.5	0.1
1850	49.9	10.5	2.2	8.4	6.7	21.2	0.1

Sources: Data from Woodbine Parish, *Buenos Ayres and the Provinces of the Rio de la Plata,* 2d ed. (London, 1852), 520; and from Miron Burgin, *The Economic Aspects of Argentine Federalism 1820–1852* (Cambridge, MA, 1946), 49, 167, 198.

1840 to 29.6 million, 71 percent, in 1841. For the rest of the regime it never fell below 15 million, or 49 percent (see Table 5.1).

This was the system of total government that sustained Rosas in power for over two decades. It proclaimed a sole truth in politics and demanded exclusive allegiance. The majority of the people obeyed, some with enthusiasm, some from inertia, many out of fear. Was the regime a precursor of modern totalitarianism, or was it something more primitive? Most outside observers saw it simply as the despotism of one man: "The character of General Rosas is impressed on every act and every word that comes from authority. His intervention descends to the minutia of dress and the daily habits of the people. He aims at establishing a thorough patriarchal system of despotic rule, which is borne in silence and religiously obeyed, but not without much secret discontent and ill will."[21]

Rosas's tyranny was, however, not arbitrarily imposed. His government responded to conditions inherent in Argentine society, where men had lived for too long without a common power to keep them all in awe. Rosas superseded a state of nature, when life was a war of every man against every man, and when people and their leaders lived with continual fear and the danger of violent death. He offered an escape from insecurity and a promise of peace, on condition that he be granted total power, the sole antidote to total anarchy. This he received by irrevocable consent. For Buenos Aires, this was the generation of the great leviathan, and Rosas the mortal god. His power conformed in many respects to the concept of sovereignty in Thomas Hobbes: "For by this Authoritie, given him by every particular man in the Common-Wealth, he hath the use of so much Power and Strength conferred on him, that by terror thereof, he is inabled to forme the wills of them all, to Peace at home, and mutuall ayd against their enemies abroad."[22] From the time he was installed in office, Rosas held the classical rights of sovereignty in all their Hobbesian purity—the right to immunity from deposition, dissent, criticism, and punishment; the power of life and death; the right to use all means to preserve peace and security for all; the power to prescribe laws concerning the rights of persons and property; the right of judicature; the right to make peace and war on other nations; the right to impose taxes; the right to choose his own ministers, magistrates, and officials; the power of rewarding, punishing, and granting honors. All these rights were inseparable, and there was no division of powers. To exercise this sovereignty, Rosas used the bureaucracy, the military, and the police. And in reserve he held another constraint, terror.

6

THE TERROR

Enemies of Rosas

Opposition to Rosas was insistent but fragmented; with enclaves at home, in the provinces, abroad, his enemies could pose a threat only in association. Their disunity was his opportunity: to survive he had to concentrate overwhelming power on one front at a time and avoid a general conflagration. The most vulnerable dissidents were the nearest. They were mainly an ideological opposition, partly unitarians and partly younger reformists; their resistance came to a head in an abortive conspiracy in 1839 and continued to operate from its base in Montevideo.

A second focus of internal opposition was formed by the landowners of the south of the province. As the justice of the peace of Chascomús reported, "Commandant Rico was at the head of a considerable armed force in support of the insurrection led by Don Benito Miguens and Don Pedro Castelli. A number of hacendados were accomplices in the rebellion. . . . The whole extent of the country as far as Bahía Blanca was roused to the insurrection."[1] The rebels issued a statement to the French admiral Louis Leblanc, upholding the principles of liberty and the cause of Lavalle and the Argentines against the tyranny of Rosas and appealing to the French alliance in the common struggle, but not for French conquest and occupation, as Rosas alleged.[2] Opposition stemmed not from ideology but from economic interest. Already harassed by demands on their manpower and resources for the Indian frontier, the southerners were particularly hit by the French blockade, which cut off their export outlets and for which they held Rosas responsible. But the rebellion of October 1839 did not synchronize with the political conspiracy, and it too was crushed.

Finally, there was external opposition to the regime, partly from other provinces and partly from foreign powers. If this opposition could link with internal dissidents, Rosas would be in real danger. To oppose Rosas, of course, was a crime for which there was no reprieve. He lived in personal anticipation of danger, and in 1839, fear of assassination was a daily obsession. One of his secretariat reported:

> The dictator is not stupid: he knows the people hate him; he goes in constant fear and always has one eye on the chance to rob and abuse them and the other on making a getaway. He has a horse ready saddled at the door of his office day and night; I am not exaggerating, there is an Indian appointed solely as his bodyguard. . . . From rising to retiring Rosas is spurred, whip in hand, with hat and poncho, always ready to mount his horse. He strikes me as a man who while murdering someone to rob him is constantly looking round at the slightest noise.[3]

State Terrorism

Rosas did not rest on defensive measures. He counterattacked. He used terror as an instrument of government to eliminate enemies, discipline dissidents, warn waverers, and ultimately control his own supporters. Terrorism was not popular, spontaneous, or indiscriminate. Such a tactic would have been uncharacteristic of the regime, which prided itself on maintaining law and order. As to personal security, observers agreed, Buenos Aires was one of the safest places in the world. So terror was not anarchic. Nor was it a delegated power, fashioned and applied by subordinates. The agents of the terror were not its authors; they did not make the policy or choose the victims. In this regime the government was the terrorist. That was why the machinery of terror could be turned on and off with such precision. Terror was not massive or continuous but limited and sporadic. And it was not an instrument of class. Within its essentially political objectives, there was a certain class bias, for the principal victims were the unitarian elite; but this policy was strategic rather than social, intended to destroy a rival ruling class. Terror was applied to people and groups carefully selected by the government. It was considered pointless to kill poor and insignificant people. And the terrorists did not touch foreigners, even during the French and

Anglo-French blockades. Usually the victims were directly or indirectly, rightly or wrongly, linked to the unitarian cause, and when the terrorists could not lay hands on unitarians, they took, in effect, a substitute or equivalent for the demonstration value. Apart from unitarians, some of the targets were political and administrative groups that Rosas could not dispense with but in which he had little confidence. Terror was also a sinister warning to others in the regime from a ruler who sought unconditional docility in his servants and who was determined to dominate his movement and destroy factions.

Terror also had a military dimension; it was applied on the battlefield. Armies were exterminated; prisoners were rarely taken or, if taken, were then killed; fugitives were hunted down, their throats cut, their heads exhibited. Savagery was cultivated as a deterrent to frighten off potential opposition; terrorism became an accompaniment, sometimes an alternative, to battles. Terror, therefore, was not simply a series of exceptional episodes, though it was regulated according to circumstances. It was an intrinsic part of the Rosas system, the distinctive style of the regime. It marked the vengeance and the power of Rosas; it was a punishment for the past and a warning for the future. Terror was the ultimate sanction of the Rosas state, the final coercion.

Terrorism flowed from the extraordinary powers vested in Rosas. Alternative methods were available, for the normal machinery of justice still existed. But Rosas bypassed the law's process and dispensed summary justice, especially during times of internal crisis and national emergency. He could never forget that he had the sole power of life and death, that he could judge the accused without trial, that his word was sufficient to send a man to the executioner. Foreigners such as the British minister John Henry Mandeville were astonished by the extent and the application of his personal sovereignty: "What I blame him for is, his having them [the executed] shot by soldiers, when the executioner ought to be the performer, authorised by the sentence of the proper tribunal, which he, since I have been here, has in all cases dispensed with. Some are shot onboard a little ten gun brig lying in the roads, some in one barrack, some in another, without any of them as I am informed, going through the ordinary forms of justice or judgement."[4]

Cases concerning political security and rural order were the particular business of Rosas and came directly to him. A typical month, November 1835, provides a number of examples. Gregorio Barragón, a unitarian who became violent in prison, was sentenced to be shot at 10 o'clock one morning in the square at Navarro. Toribio González, twenty-five years old, was sentenced by Rosas to be shot at 10 o'clock in the morning in the square of Lobos. Santiago Carvajas, thirty-five years old, accused of robbery in a pulpería at Lobos, was shot in the main square. Through such punishments, Rosas ruled the south of the province, which he regarded as an extension of his private estates. Elsewhere his administration of justice was hardly less informal. From Santos Lugares, Antonino Reyes, his chief secretary at headquarters, sent him lists of criminals, unitarians, and deserters, and Rosas simply wrote "shoot him" or "flog him" and so on down the list. Some of these cases were purely political; others were criminal matters of vagrancy, robbery, assault, and murder. In either category a man could be shot without trial, and the unitarian delinquent was almost certainly doomed. In these prosecutions, a combination of political witch-hunting and maintaining rural security, there was no sign of police evidence or any judicial process. The executive was judge and executioner, acting by virtue of his extraordinary powers.

The penal system was bloody in Argentina, whatever the regime. To Sarmiento, intent on depicting Rosas as unoriginal as well as uncivilized, the difference appeared one of degree: "Rosas invented nothing; his talent was only to copy his predecessors and turn the brutal instinct of the ignorant masses into a cold and calculated system."[5] Cruelty is difficult to measure, and in the writings of the time, propaganda often prevailed over precision. Nevertheless, the rule of Rosas left an ineffaceable impression of bloodshed and death. The prisons were probably more oppressive and the executions more gruesome than those of his predecessors. In the south of the province some of the prisons were really private hacienda gaols. The most notorious prisons were in the capital: the Cuartel de Serenos, ruled by Colonel Nicolás Mariño; the Cuartel de Cuitiño in the calle Chacabuco; the Cuartel de Restauradores on the corner of the calles Defensa and México; and of course Santos Lugares, the military headquarters of the regime. For many people, to enter these doors was to enter a death cell.

The modes of execution, however, were not invented by Rosas and were not peculiar to one side. The knife and the lance were part of the cultural heritage of Argentina, ingrained in creole and gaucho tradition. Rosas inherited his modes of execution in part from the rural environment, in part from prevailing laws. There were three principal methods: shooting, lance thrust, and throat-cutting. The most characteristic procedure was throat-cutting; this was the favored punishment and the most valued technique. The knife was the gaucho's weapon and to cut a throat, his delight. As Hudson recalled: "The people of the plains had developed an amazing ferocity, they loved to kill a man not with a bullet but in a manner to make them know and feel that they were really and truly killing."[6] But what may be attributed to a cultural flaw in a primitive creature of the pampas becomes an abuse of power in the hands of the state. Sarmiento was probably correct in suggesting that Rosas carried this practice further than others: "Execution by cutting the throat with a knife instead of by shooting, is the result of the butcher's instinct which Rosas has exploited to give executions a more gaucho-like form and more pleasure to the assassins; above all, to change the legal punishments recognised by civilised societies for others, which he calls American."[7]

The terror of this regime was extraordinary even by the standards of the time. The diarist Juan Manuel Beruti recorded an incident of particular savagery: "Benitez, a man of over sixty, did not have his throat cut; instead he was left alive but incapacitated. For the throat-cutter, Alem, staked him out on four posts, face upwards and about half a yard off the ground. He then placed a brazier of fire underneath him and burnt his testicles and intestines. . . . All this I have copied from the public records, and it is only an extract."[8] The atmosphere of terror that prevailed served the regime almost as much as the killings themselves. During the peak of terrorism in October 1840, headless bodies were found in Buenos Aires every morning; for the terrorists the demonstration was as important as the deed. It was common practice among the military to stick the heads of victims on long poles and display them in public squares. Violence was reflected in the language of the time. *Degollar, degollador,* these were among the commonest words in the vocabulary of rosismo, and they were used with a depraved pleasure by ruler and followers alike.

The Mazorca

The agents of terrorism were members of the Sociedad Popular Restaurador, a political club and a parapolice organization. The society had an armed wing, commonly called the mazorca. The word "mazorca," meaning "a head of maize," symbolized strength through union, but it really gained currency because it sounded the same as "mas horca," or "more hanging." According to some, it had an even more horrifying connotation: "The Mashorca, or secret affiliation in support of Rosas' government, derives its name from the inward stalk of the maize, when deprived of its grain, and has been used by the members of the club as an instrument of torture of which your lordship may have some idea when calling to mind the agonising death inflicted upon Edward II."[9] At patriotic feasts federal fanatics would jump to their feet and cry out against a unitarian, "Here is a toasted maize; let us put it where he deserves it."

The Sociedad Popular Restaurador first emerged as an organization for Rosas during the struggle against the federal dissidents in 1832–1833. Under the patronage of Doña Encarnación its leaders were placed on the state payroll and specialized in intimidating political adversaries. A squad of activists would ride through Buenos Aires, fire shots at houses, frighten off enemies, and drive out dissidents to Entre Ríos or Uruguay. At the end of April 1834, intimidation increased: Rivadavia had returned to Buenos Aires, and the activists sought to expulse him with pressure and violence. The society was born, therefore, as a pressure group for Rosas and an instrument of political extortion while he was out of office. It then became a terrorist agency, a kind of vigilantes group, when he returned to office. But it was not a wholly private organization. It was part spontaneous, part official; in a sense, it institutionalized terror and controlled violence, thus avoiding the things most abhorrent to Rosas—anarchy, mob rule, and personal vendetta. It is doubtful that it was genuinely popular; it had no power of its own independent of Rosas, and it shared none of his sovereignty. It was not a committee of public safety, Jacobin club, or political party, descriptions that it has sometimes received. It was essentially a paramilitary or parapolice organization. It was a select and exclusive body, difficult to enter because qualification for membership was by services rendered, not by a passive federalism.

The leader of the society, Julián González Salomón, claimed a special relationship with Rosas, a confidential one in his own view, an obsequious one by any objective standard. In September 1840, he described the Sociedad Popular Restaurador, in language as violent as that of its followers, as "the strong support of the cause which Your Excellency so worthily sustains," dedicated to "exterminating" the savage unitarians and any other opponents whom Rosas might indicate. Rosas's reply demonstrated his close link with the society: "That is very satisfactory in my view. . . . In due course I will ask you to come and talk, meanwhile get in touch with Manuelita for advice."[10]

Not all members of the Sociedad Popular Restaurador were active terrorists. There was a functional division into two sections, the majority of the society and the mazorca. The society was the brain, the mazorca the arm. The society helped to compile the lists of suspects; the mazorca were the activists who hauled them in. The society demonstrated for Rosas's policy; the mazorca applied it. The elite of the society, upper-class members who often joined simply as insurance, urged or tolerated terrorism but did not themselves gallop around Buenos Aires cutting throats. That was left to the shock troops, the mazorca. The mazorqueros were the true terrorists, recruited from sectors lower than the rosista elite and forming armed squads that went out on various missions. They conducted house-to-house searches, destroying everything blue and intimidating the owners; they acted on police reports such as "he has not given any service to the Federation and dresses like a unitarian"; they arrested; they tortured; and they killed. Nothing was sacred. The mazorca even terrorized the assembly: "The mazorca brandished their knives in the very galleries of the House of Representatives, and their fierce and sarcastic threats could be heard everywhere."[11] It was difficult to evade the system, for it had many eyes and a long reach. The society supplied, in effect, a network of spies, agents, and informers as well as the death squads. It was the guardian of pure federalism, the shield of the regime and its knife.

Who were these militants for Rosas? There was no secret about the membership of the Sociedad Popular Restaurador. It consisted in 1842 of some 200 people whose names were proudly published in the *Gaceta Mercantil*. They were, according to the historian

Adolfo Saldías, "fanatical supporters, military of all ranks, men well
known in society, in the administration, in letters, and in the law."[12]
Not surprisingly, they included members of the House of
Representatives and other elite groups who joined as much out of
fear as conviction. The president was Julián González Salomón, a
native of Buenos Aires, owner of a pulpería, a man gross in body and
mind. This society was the political side of the movement. The
mazorca, the superterrorists, were recruited from lower social
groups, often from the police and the *serenos* (corps of nightwatch-
men), and they included professional cutthroats and delinquents.
Their leaders were the notorious and sinister pair Ciriaco Cuitiño
and Andrés Parra, killers and organizers of killing, former militia
officers and clients of Rosas. In addition to leading the death squads,
they could also raise and manipulate a mob, another of their functions. The Buenos Aires mob was not a spontaneous or independent
force. It too was a creature of Rosas, as outsiders appreciated: "[The
mob] must not be understood here in its usual sense, but as hirelings
of the police."[13]

The Sociedad Popular Restaurador and its armed wing were created, sanctioned, and controlled by Rosas. The mazorca was a force
of urban irregulars who were on the state payroll and received secret
service money. It was not a department of state but worked closely
with official bodies such as the police and the corps of nightwatch-
men, and there was evidently a degree of joint membership. Orders
for specific executions, moreover, were given to mazorca leaders verbally by Rosas; so Cuitiño later claimed, and there is no reason to
doubt it. However, although the mazorca was a creature of Rosas, it
was more terrorist than its creator. Like many such death squads, it
acquired in action a semiautonomy, and once it was on the streets,
it was not amenable to absolute control in every detail. It would be
untrue to say that Rosas had unleashed a tiger he could not control.
But although he gave precise instructions for executions and chose
the victims carefully, he could not curb every killing beyond the official list. Still, if he did not personally order every act of terror, he
could have stopped excesses. He seems to have known that the
mazorca went not against but further than his orders. He believed
that he could not govern without the mazorca and that he had to
allow it a measure of licence. The terror thus acquired a momentum
of its own and became a tolerated tyranny.

Stages of Terror

Cruelty had its chronology. The incidence of terrorism varied according to the pressures on the regime, rising to a peak in 1839–1842, when French intervention, internal rebellion, and unitarian invasion threatened to destroy the Rosas state and produced violent countermeasures. The peak of 1839–1842 was not typical of the whole regime but rather an extraordinary manifestation of a general rule, namely that terrorism existed to enforce submission to government methods in times of national emergency.

Terrorism began during the first administration of Rosas, when the killing of Captain Juan José Montero became a cause célèbre and set the style of government to come. Montero was a tough and turbulent Chilean officer of Indian origin, a veteran of the liberating expedition across the Andes and subsequently of the Indian frontier, where he served in the garrison of Bahía Blanca. At the beginning of 1829, when the agents of Rosas were raising rural contingents for war against the unitarians, Montero preferred to lead his Indians to Lavalle's support and subsequently resisted Rosas's orders to bring himself and his Indians into the federal camp. Rosas did not forget, and when he was elected governor, he had an opportunity to settle the score. In 1830, he summoned Montero and gave him a letter to take to Colonel Prudencio Rosas, who without trial or explanation had the officer shot. The letter carried by Montero contained the order for his execution.

The Montero case might be considered an isolated incident were it not for two aspects that gave it a wider significance. First, it had macabre and sensational features that were to become the hallmark of rosista terrorism. Second, it drew from Rosas an explanation of his power as he interpreted it, for the killing undoubtedly embarrassed his friends and outraged his enemies. Rosas became aware that he was acquiring a reputation as a killer, but he rejected the imputation. He maintained that Montero was executed not for his political opinions but as a criminal, and he justified the action by virtue of his extraordinary powers, giving in the process an interpretation showing how they could be invoked to justify terrorism: "The law which gave me authority is the law which ordered Montero to be killed. It will be said that I abused the power. If this is so, it will be my error but not a crime to cause me remorse. Because when I

was given this hateful extraordinary power I was given it not on condition that I always had to be right but to act with complete freedom, according to my judgement, and to act without restrictions,
for the sole object of saving the dying country."[14] What he described
was a terrorist's charter.

At the beginning of Rosas's second government, between 1835
and 1839, the executions could be described as normal routine. For
the most part, due legal processes were observed; in cases of assassination and robbery, sentences were severe, but they were given by the
courts and applied by the police. Yet there were premonitions of the
terror to come. In May 1835 three military personnel, alleged conspirators against Rosas's life, were executed without trial, an inaugu-
ral sacrifice, as it were, that temporarily satisfied Rosas. There were
Indian victims, too, some seventy or so Araucanians brought in 1836
in chains from the frontier and shot ten at a time in front of the Buen
Retiro barracks without the semblance of a trial. Violence against
frontier Indians was regarded as warfare, not terror, and in the execution of prisoners of war, Rosas did not discriminate between whites
and Indians; anyone taken in battle was at risk. The assassination of
Facundo Quiroga drew a measured response from Rosas. He asserted
his interprovincial prerogative and brought the Reinafé brothers and
other accused to trial in Buenos Aires. They were sentenced to death
and executed on October 25, 1837, and their corpses were hung
under the arches of the cabildo, leaving an image of the regime for art
and letters to record. Yet in retrospect, these were tranquil years, ago-
nizing for some, no doubt, but secure enough for those who kept
their heads down. Terrorism lurked but was not yet rampant. The
year 1838 was the turning point, the time when external shock was
followed by prolonged reverberations within.

The French blockade of Buenos Aires from March 1838 to
October 1840 created classical conditions for terrorism. Economic
stagnation, an official austerity program, and political tension
severely tested the Rosas state and produced strains at various points.
As the weak links appeared in the capital, in the south, and in the
provinces, the government struck back hard to repair the damage.
The first target was in the provinces. Rosas believed that the most
immediate danger came from the governor of Santa Fe, Domingo
Cullen. First, Rosas instigated a rebellion against him in Santa Fe and
drove him out, then he extracted him from the sanctuary in Santiago

del Estero provided by Governor Felipe Ibarra, and finally he had him brought back. At the end of the long road, on June 22, 1839, Cullen barely had time to write to his wife—"They have just told me I have to die"—and bid her look after their twelve children.[15] Then, at the foot of an ombu tree in Arroyo del Medio, the escort bound his eyes and shot him; the orders came from Rosas, and there was no trial.

The conspirators in Buenos Aires felt at one with Cullen and were sympathetic observers of his fate. They themselves, an underground group of young reformists who planned to overthrow Rosas in alliance with dissident military officers, were already under observation by the dictator, and in his own time he pounced. The mazorca moved into action, whipping up its mob to intimidate anyone suspected of belonging to the unitarian or French party and to attack Dr. Manuel Vicente Maza, president of the House of Representatives and of the supreme court of justice, a former supporter of the ideas and actions of Rosas but now linked to the conspiracy through his son Colonel Ramón Maza. Instead of a trial and a great repression, Rosas decided on summary justice against a few. The father was assassinated by the mazorca in the House of Representatives on June 27, 1839. The son was shot without trial in the prison patio on the following day. The widow committed suicide. Rosas disclaimed all responsibility for the assassination of the father but regarded the execution of the son as a legitimate action of government. These sombre events inaugurated a great fear in Buenos Aires, and the streets became silent and empty.

The third focus of rebellion lay in the south, and it too failed. The defeat of the hacendados was followed by a hard but concentrated repression. Pedro Castelli was hunted down and killed while resisting arrest. He was then decapitated, and on the orders of Rosas, "so that his colleagues might see the condign punishment sent from heaven," his head was sent to Dolores and stuck on a pole in the main square. Excesses were committed by the government troops in the south, following their victory. Many captives were brought in chains to Buenos Aires and led through the streets to prison. Most of these were spared, however, some on the intercession of the British minister. On the whole, only the leaders of the rebellion were executed. A similar distinction was made in the following year in the execution of prisoners from Lavalle's invading army.

Lavalle did not synchronize his invasion with the internal rebellions. He led his forces into the province of Buenos Aires on August 5, 1840, but lost his nerve and withdrew on September 6. Fiasco though it was, the invasion gave Rosas a shock. He decreed the expropriation of unitarian property and prepared to employ the terrorist's knife to deter defectors and to eliminate the enemy within. The first victims at hand were the invaders, or the stragglers among them. Rosas gave instructions that those who wished to join the federal forces, especially the poor, should be accepted. "But His Excellency says that this does not apply to the rich or to those called decent, for none of these are good; therefore all those who belong to this class of savages should be shot or have their throats cut immediately."[16]

The Great Terror: 1840

During 1840 with an enemy army still at large and a traitor imagined in every barrio, Rosas ordered out his death squads. In Buenos Aires, killings increased in numbers and in virulence as the government hunted its numerous targets. To seek safety in flight was taken as admission of guilt, and those who fled were seen as the enemy or as potential recruits. On May 4 a group of men with reason to believe they were on the mazorca's list attempted to escape to Uruguay. They were Colonel Francisco Lynch, Carlos Masón, José María Riglos, and Isidoro Oliden, and they had arranged to have a boat ready at night in a place near the British minister's house. But they were watched, and as they approached the embarkation point, they were surrounded by a mazorca squad and their throats were cut. According to Cuitiño, the orders for these executions came verbally from Rosas to Colonel Parra. The killings continued sporadically and eventually reached their peak not during the worst of the emergency but after the withdrawal of Lavalle's army. By then the Maza conspiracy had been eradicated, the rebellion of the south defeated, Lavalle outmaneuvered, and the French brought to the peace table. But if the worst of the crisis was over, the worst of the terror was still to come.

What, then, was the explanation of terrorism? Was it a means of immediate national defense, or was it a precaution against the future? Was it invoked as the only method of government equal to the emergency, or was it a calculated vengeance once the emergency had passed? Was it imposed by the logic of events, or was it the cruel choice of its creator? Was terror a defense against the enemy, or could it be employed with impunity only when the enemy had withdrawn? The terror of Rosas contained an element of all these things, without a simple rationale. But however peculiar the timing, the intention was clear enough—to destroy those whose loyalty was suspect, to strengthen the security of the state, and to ensure political subordination.

The terror of 1840 was presented as a popular and spontaneous explosion. In fact, it was officially inspired, and it was administered by a small group of men directly or indirectly in the pay of the state, mainly police and the mazorca. Moreover, terrorism was carefully measured and the victims were precisely chosen, for an indiscriminate massacre might well have provoked a mass reaction. The prime targets of the terrorists were unitarians, real or alleged, and a number of people within the federal ranks who were regarded as a security risk. Guilt was retrospective and anticipated. It was also fatal. According to General Antonio Díaz, "The bloody scenes of October 1840 have their origin in the threats and protests of vengeance issued (according to General Rosas) by General Lavalle; but we believe that the true object was to ensure by means of the terror the loyalty of those of his subordinates whose determination he thought he could see weakening at the approach of Lavalle, including even his own brothers."[17] Many unitarians were helplessly incriminated by the simple fact of having relatives in Lavalle's army, as the British minister noted: "Although there is not a general rising in favour of Lavalle, he has a strong party in his favour, and the misery and distress occasioned by the blockade are daily making . . . enemies against the present government. The town is compressed with terror and appears like an abandoned city, for most of the labouring people have been forced to join the army, and many of the middling and upper classes, having relations in General Lavalle's army, fear to leave their houses and appear in public."[18]

At the peak of the crisis, Rosas was in his military headquarters at Santos Lugares, as though to remain aloof from the city, whose government he delegated to Arana. The chief of police, Bernardo Victorica, reported regularly to Rosas; acting under orders, he and his squads hunted down unitarians throughout the city. Numerous suspects were detained, some 250 at the time of Lavalle's invasion. For five weeks, from September 23 to October 27, 1840, Buenos Aires was at the mercy of the terrorists. People kept to their houses, shuttered their windows, and locked their doors, and the streets of the capital, sombre at the best of times, became yet more lifeless, silent, and deserted. The only movement in the streets was that of the terrorists, groups of mazorqueros in red ponchos, some in high-crowned hats with a federal band, some in peaked caps, and all armed with guns or knives or truncheons. They hunted their quarry through the streets or invaded houses. And each morning neighbors asked each other, how many throats cut, how many corpses? People had to guard their speech, especially in front of their servants, for to be denounced was like a death sentence: *la tiranía estaba en los de abajo.* This was the pattern of events, not a massacre but a succession of individual assassinations.

In addition to killing, the terrorists also attacked the property of unitarians; on the pretext of searching for fugitives and arms, they burst into houses, beating up the inhabitants, robbing, and destroying. The correct forms were not entirely discarded: one of the procedures, whereby the police asked a judge for a search warrant authorizing the mazorca to enter houses in pursuit of unitarian fugitives, clearly illustrated the link between officials and terrorists. And behind it all was Rosas, distant yet present, the prime mover and the first terrorist. He subsequently described the terror as "the laudable and ardent expression of vehement patriotism" and a manifestation of "popular excitement." But his own officials, Victorica and Cuitiño, stated that Rosas made the decisions and gave them their orders. This was state terrorism.

In due course the British minister protested. Mandeville was sympathetic to Rosas and usually gave him the benefit of the doubt, which perhaps makes his evidence of the terror the more convincing. The immediate reason for his intervention was the increasing proximity of the violence, but he took the opportunity to generalize and to warn Rosas of the dangerous level of terrorism. On the previous night, he wrote on October 9, "a group of people broke the windows of a number of houses in the block next to the one where I live; they then attacked the house opposite mine, and shouting death to the inhabitants broke the windows and tried to break down the doors with rubble and stones." He reminded Rosas that this was "the residence of a foreign minister, representative of a nation friendly to his country, which should be immune from a wild mob rampaging in its immediate vicinity." He had been advised, moreover, that his own life was in danger and he should not go out at night.[19]

Rosas replied immediately and at some length. Although he promised Mandeville adequate guard for the legation, he was unrepentant, indeed defiant, about the terror. He justified the conduct of the mob by reason of "the extraordinary circumstances in which this unfortunate country has been placed through the cruelties of its barbarous enemies." He also implied that the British were not blameless, as the minister was known to have made special pleas for individual unitarians and his compatriots to have helped others to escape. Rosas argued that he could not go beyond public opinion, could not stop the federal fury; otherwise he would alienate the very supporters whom he needed to govern and to prevent anarchy. "Do not imagine that I have sufficient power to remedy here and now these misfortunes. . . . Such measures would only cause greater resentment." And as long as the English were hostile, was it surprising if the people turned nasty? "If this happens, I will not be able to answer for the security of property and persons, not even those of the English."[20]

In his letter to Mandeville, Rosas gave the impression that the events of October 1840 were the natural and spontaneous reaction of the popular masses against the savage unitarians and that to stop this upsurge was more than his government dared do. This was the official version of the terror. It was also, in a sense, true, but it was not the whole truth. There was always a danger of anarchical terror. Any government that creates and uses an illicit instrument of violence has to give the monster its head and allow it to prowl freely. As he believed that he could not govern without terror, Rosas had to give scope to the terrorists. But in the final count the terror of Rosas was directed and controlled from above, starting at the top, through the mazorca, and down to those whom it cared to mobilize. As Mandeville concluded, "There is an occult power more powerful than the Government, but which can be controlled by the hand that directs it, if interest or inclination prompts it to do so."[21] Rosas did not have to issue personally a continuous series of directives in order to control terrorism. He simply had to remain at a distance and do nothing to stop it until he was ready to do so, the normal method of sanctioning operations of this kind. There is no doubt that he approved of what was done: "It is necessary to purge the Republic of such traitors. . . . They must feel the consequences of their iniquity in their persons and their property."[22]

The killings lasted about a month, ending on October 27 and claiming some twenty victims, not all of them unitarians. On October 29, Rosas signed the convention that reestablished relations with France, and it was ratified two days later. On the same day, October 31, Rosas issued a decree justifying the terror and also ending it. The popular anger caused by the invasion of Lavalle, he explained, had erupted in "natural vengeance" that was impossible to restrain without impugning the patriotism and loyalty of the people. Now there was peace with France and greater security. The decree, therefore, imposed the penalty of death for robbery and assault and classified as disturber of the peace "any individual, of any class, who attacks the person or property of an Argentine or foreigners, without the express written order of the competent authority." This measure curbed the killers and proved not so much that Rosas could suspend the terror if he wished but that he could suspend it when he judged the time appropriate. And terror was not extinguished in Argentina; it merely shifted its ground.

In 1841, Rosas's position improved. Peace with France restored prosperity to Buenos Aires: the port was again crowded with vessels, and exports revived. The defeat of the League of the North in the course of 1841 placed the interior of the country at the mercy of Rosas. His army under Manuel Oribe imposed in one blow the reign of terror that in Buenos Aires had gradually built up to the peak of 1840. Hitherto the interior provinces had not experienced terror on this scale; now it was inflicted on them in a bloody, barbarous, and remorseless campaign by a rosista military applying a policy sanctioned by its master.

The Great Terror: 1842

In the course of 1841, terror remained in abeyance in Buenos Aires. But Rosas continued to intervene in the judicial process and to dispense summary justice; the police files for the years 1840–1842 contained many more personal orders from Rosas than previously, such as "shoot him," "imprison him," sometimes with cause given, sometimes without. Moreover, two developments were ominous for the future. The first was an alleged assassination plot against Rosas, comic in its details though seriously exploited by the regime. On March 23, 1841, a *máquina infernal* was discovered; this explosive device was sent in the guise of a gift from Montevideo and was intended for Rosas but opened by Manuela. According to official descriptions, it consisted of a large box filled with loaded pistols arranged to fire when opened; if these reports were true, the contraption would have killed its makers before it ever reached Rosas. The conspirators were alleged to be José Rivera Indarte and other unitarians. Skeptical observers claimed that the incident was too stupid to be taken seriously, but the regime denounced it as a dangerous and criminal act. It was the occasion for an extraordinary session of the House of Representatives, where the "horrible event" was condemned, and for public ceremonies celebrating the safe deliverance of Rosas.

The second development was the announcement by the unitarians of a hard-line policy that was just as uncompromising as that of the federalists. There had always been a terrorist element in the unitarian camp, and it too had contributed to the growth of organized violence since 1810, culminating in the deposition and killing of Governor Dorrego in December 1828 and a year of mutual reprisals. This outrage was the real beginning of terrorism, which mounted as each side practiced calculated retaliation. In the campaigns of 1840–1841 the unitarians executed federalist prisoners. In Entre Ríos, Lavalle proclaimed, "It is necessary to cut the throats of them all. Let us purge society of these monsters. Death, death without pity." These sentiments were not confined to the soldiers. From Chile, Sarmiento wrote: "It is necessary to employ terror to win the war. . . . All means are good." The message of the *comisión argentina* in Chile to the chief of the League of the North was equally chilling, urging the killing of all those who took up arms on the side of Rosas: "All methods of achieving our ends are good. . . . The greatest truth in politics is that the means are always justified by the end." The next step in the argument was inevitable, and Rivera Indarte took it: "It will be a great and holy action to kill Rosas."[23] Terror now fed upon itself as each side responded inexorably to the other. The unitarians called the federalists barbarians; the federalists called the unitarians savages. The scene was set for a new wave of terror.

As 1842 advanced, so did terrorism. With enemy troops under Rivera and Paz in Entre Ríos and alleged conspiracies against the life of Rosas in the capital, executions began to increase both in town and at Santos Lugares in the course of February. A number of prisoners of war and civilians were executed, and depression settled over Buenos Aires once more. Yet the position of Rosas, though dangerous, was not desperate, and again the timing of terror was not self-evident. The immediate threat came from Uruguay and its unitarian allies in Santa Fe and Entre Ríos; this time there was not a powerful European backer, but diplomatic hostility from Britain and France was part of the picture. The federal forces, however, converged on Santa Fe, and in the course of April 12–18 they defeated the unitarians; Entre Ríos rose against Paz on April 4 and forced him to retreat. So the coalition of Rivera, Paz, and Ferré was already in pieces when the terror reached its peak during April 11–19. The pattern of events was not so obvious to Rosas; the unitarians were defeated but not destroyed, and he was aware of Anglo-French hostility and possible intervention in the future. He therefore decided to launch a preemptive terror, to purge the body politic and strengthen security in advance. This decision is a possible explanation of the terror of April 1842. Another was advanced by General Díaz: "No one could see any object or reason in the executions of April 1842, until one night Rosas himself asked one of the persons for whom he had some regard if he had read a decree of the governor of Corrientes stating that for every unitarian killed in Buenos Aires, ten federalist prisoners would be shot. 'Now you see what those savage unitarians are; they kill and then they are afraid to die; now they will see what I think of their threats; let them make decrees and I will answer them as they deserve.' "[24]

The terror now reached its climax. In the last days of March each morning at dawn, corpses were found with their throats cut in various parts of the capital, and this carnage continued into April. Many of these killings were surrounded by mystery and committed at night. Others took place during the day. Two or three men would walk up to a victim in the street or in his house and shoot him at point-blank range or seize him and cut his throat; they would then leave unmolested while those nearby averted their faces. Assassins operated with impunity at dances, in homes and offices, and on public thoroughfares.

By the third week of April the city was petrified; the streets were empty after five or six o'clock, and the terrified inhabitants kept to their houses while outside the death squads ruled. But the killing was not indiscriminate. Mandeville, who was unable to explain the terror in a time of relative security and who appeared to be more complacent about it than previously, reported a visit to Government House: "A few nights ago I was at the Governor's house, and I asked one of the Secret Committee of the Mazhorca Club, now called *'Sociedad Popular,'* if I had not better have one man, at least, with me at night, as I live at a remote part of the town, and seldom stay at home at night. He replied no, you are as safe as Doña Manuelita, the Governor's daughter. Perhaps so, I said, when they know me, but they could make a mistake—*'Nunca se equivoca'* was his answer—there is never a mistake."[25]

If the victims were carefully chosen, they were also carefully treated; they were not usually robbed, for the terrorists wished to make it clear that these were political assassinations and not delinquency. It was a frightening lesson, especially for anyone who had had the slightest connection with unitarians. Mandeville thought that this time the intention was to drive the unitarians right out of the country and confiscate their property. But beyond the unitarians many federalists were at risk too, and apart from the federalists, others were suspect simply because they were apolitical. Soldiers, officials, leading citizens, and ordinary people were all at risk. A mute hysteria possessed Buenos Aires in April 1842, and there was a danger that terror might produce not security but instability. Foreigners were arming themselves, European consuls threatened to leave, Mandeville and other representatives protested. At this point, on April 19, the government ordered an end to the killings, and the chief of police was instructed to establish patrols to apprehend and imprison assassins. It was noticed that included in some of these patrols were men who had previously been in the death squads.

The existence of terror could not be denied; only the responsibility was disputed. Official spokesmen stated that "not thousands, nor hundreds, but forty or so" had been killed, the victims of "an indignant people."[26] Rosas claimed that he had no idea of the extent of the excesses. His order to the chief of police ending the terror spoke of his "deep disgust" at the recent assassinations; he declared that no one was authorized to exercise such license, even against unitarians; and he rebuked the police for their inertia and dereliction of duty. Yet in 1842, as in 1840, Rosas bore the ultimate responsibility for terrorism. The evidence from Mandeville's conversation with terrorists at Government House points unmistakably to official sanction. But Rosas felt that once he had activated the terror, he must allow it to run its course. There was a sense in which he had to condone excesses beyond what he authorized. In a revealing interview with Mandeville, he explained his power and its delineations:

> It is only by going along with my Party, at times, that I retain my influence with them, and that I can govern them. When the murders were going on in the frightful manner you witnessed in the month of April, at two in the afternoon of one day I issued the Orders which my Aide de Camp General Corbalan brought to you—Well, they could not be made known in every part of the town at once, and what happened, Victorica, the Chief of Police, fell upon a band which had been at work, many escaped, but the chief was taken, and hung up instantly, and another shot the next morning. The people saw that I was determined to put an end to these excesses, and they yielded, but more from respect to my wishes than from fear of me, who know not fear and fears nought but God. . . . There is no aristocracy here to support a Government, public opinion and the masses govern.[27]

Prime Terrorist

The termination of the terror of April 1842 did not put an end to the repressive tendencies of the Rosas state. After 1842, terror and extraordinary violence became uncharacteristic of the regime, though it was still possible to draw swift retaliation for the slightest political offense. In 1846 the mazorca was disbanded and its members returned to legitimate posts, as the diarist Beruti recorded: "1 June 1846. From today the *sociedad popular restauradora,* alias the *mas-horca,* which has caused so much harm and so many tears, has been dissolved, and its members have been ordered to join the active-service and reserve militias, as may be appropriate."[28] Rosas no longer needed a special agency of terror: internally, if not abroad, he had overcome his enemies. Nevertheless, the regime was still based on violence, even if it was used less frequently. As Southern remarked: "The force of the government here is terror: and as the governor occupies himself with the pettiest details of daily life, is the vigilant chief of his own active police, never forgets the smallest circumstance, or forgives it, if considered an indication of hostility. Your Lordship will easily understand that we live here as it were in a great prison. By the extraordinary powers given by the Hall of Representatives, and which if not given would be taken, the governor has sole power of life and death without trial."[29] These views were recorded shortly after the most singular exercise of power in the whole regime.

The story began as melodrama and ended in tragedy. Camila O'Gorman, the nineteen-year-old daughter of a French immigrant, became acquainted with a young man from the interior, Ladislao Gutiérrez, who was persuaded by his family to enter the priesthood. He was assigned to a parish in Buenos Aires, and there, in the narrow social life of the time, it was easy for the couple to fall in love but difficult to hide it. When the hopelessness of their situation became apparent, they decided to elope and seek a new life far from the reach of church and state, perhaps even in the United States, where, they believed, "priests may marry." They fled on December 12, 1847, and reached Corrientes, hoping to live there for a time in decent obscurity as schoolteachers. Meanwhile, the church was scandalized, Rosas was furious, and the unitarians were delighted. Although later generations were impressed by the romantic appeal of the lovers' flight across the plains to the distant north, the opposition press in Montevideo and Chile exploited the elopement to taunt the regime for its want of morals. Rosas now suffered loss of face as well as an affront to his authority. But his reach was long. As soon as he received intelligence of their whereabouts, he had the couple arrested and brought back to Buenos Aires. They were imprisoned in Santos Lugares, and to the astonishment even of hardened officials and in spite of Camila's plea that she was pregnant, they were immediately sentenced to death. They were brought before a firing squad together on August 18, 1848, Camila standing tragically in white, and there they were shot.

So in the dawn, the drummers beat the call
And these poor children, wakened to be killed,
Were taken out and placed against a wall
Facing the soldiers, then the bell was stilled
That had been tolling, and a minute's space
Was given for their farewells and last embrace.

Then hand in hand they faced the firing squad,
Who shot them dead into their waiting graves.[30]

The savage sentence was the responsibility of Rosas alone. The higher clergy and the lawyers seem to have urged severity, but he subsequently denied that he was influenced by any outsider: "No one advised me to execute the priest Gutiérrez and Camila O'Gorman, nor did anyone speak to me on their behalf. On the contrary, all the leading members of the clergy spoke or wrote to me about this insolent crime and the urgent necessity to make an exemplary punishment to prevent similar scandals in the future. I thought the same. And as it was my responsibility, I ordered the execution."[31] Rosas was curiously proud of his judgment. Yet it was a new cause of alienation from his regime. According to Southern, "A panic seized the population of Buenos Ayres, and the imaginations of men were occupied in devising what would be the next act by which Rosas would mark this eventful period."[32] The diarist Beruti reflected the disquiet that the execution caused in Buenos Aires:

> These deaths caused shock and sadness among all the inhabitants of the city, for an offence which was not thought to deserve the death penalty but simply detention for a time to clear the scandal they had caused, in a simple affair of love which harmed no one, only themselves. The most lamentable aspect was that she was eight months pregnant. The governor was informed, but this gentleman ignored the innocent creature in the womb, did not wait for the mother to give birth, and ordered her to be shot. Such a thing had never happened in Buenos Aires; by killing two, three died.[33]

People were overcome not simply by sympathy for the victims but by the fear that at the very moment when normality and prosperity appeared to be at hand, Buenos Aires was returning to the terror of more barbarous times. They were reminded dramatically of the limitless power of Rosas and their own helplessness. This knowledge counted more in people's minds than the relatively few executions after 1848, mainly cases of delinquency, though desertions too drew swift retribution. Rosas defended his severity to the British minister, employing basically an argument derived from alleged socioracial differences between Europeans and Argentines:

> His Excellency then declaimed against the idea of governing in these countries by European notions; and by analyzing the character of his countrymen, that extraordinary mixture as he called it of the Spanish and the Indian character, endeavoured to convince me, that none but the severest punishments had any avail, and rarely even those: that the executions he directed were not even with the view of punishing the culprit, and scarcely in that of deterring other criminals, but simply to prevent them from again inflicting injury on society.[34]

By this time, whatever he said, the damage had been done. Rosas would go down in history as one of the cruelest of rulers as well as one of the most powerful. The subject, no doubt, has been distorted by propaganda and prejudice, but there remains an irreducible element of truth in the reputation of Rosas as a terrorist. And he earned his reputation not only from the gruesome nature of his terrorism but also from the number of its victims and his personal responsibility for their fate.

It is impossible to quantify the terror under Rosas. Contemporaries attempted to do so, but the results were flawed by bias and error. The so-called tables of blood compiled by the journalist Rivera Indarte listed 5,884 victims of terror and 16,520 killed in military action. These "opposition" figures are probably too high and fail to discriminate between delinquents and victims of political persecution, between legal punishments and assassination. In refutation the *Gaceta Mercantil* published what might be regarded as official figures: 500 executions in fourteen years, 1829–1843. Of these, it was argued, 250 took place in the provinces by order of their own governors, and a further 100 were of hostile Indians; this left 150 cases of execution, and these were unitarians guilty of conspiracy and other crimes. Other sources were less partisan but also less complete, being based on anecdotal or temporary observations. After his defeat and exile, Rosas was tried in his absence by the courts of Buenos Aires. It was a political exercise, by no means impartial, but some of the evidence for the period 1829–1852 was drawn from police archives, and the figure there of 2,354 victims, some of whom were condemned to the army rather than the firing squad, may be quoted if only to give an alternative impression.

Political executions, then, claimed a large number of victims, more than 250, less than 6,000, and perhaps in the region of 2,000 for the whole period 1829–1852. If historians are unable to measure the terror, they may nevertheless draw some conclusions. These were not mass murders. The targets were precisely chosen and carefully identified. Their impact, however, is not to be measured by quantity alone but by the suffering they inflicted on the victims' families and by the fear they instilled in the whole population. It can be assumed that Rosas calculated the amount of terror needed to produce results in wider circles beyond the victims. If ever a regime ruled by the principle of fear, it was his. Rosas acted according to a pure Hobbesian belief that fear is the only thing that makes men keep the laws. In political terms his methods worked. Terror helped keep Rosas in power and the people in order for some twenty years; it served in this regard as one of a number of factors in 1829–1832 and 1835–1838, as a major instrument of government in 1839–1842, and as a latent threat from 1843 to 1852. In this sense, terror served its purpose. But who was the prime terrorist?

Rosas was responsible for the terror: contemporaries affirmed it, and historians agree. As Mansilla remarked, "Whether Rosas ordered the throat-cutting or simply permitted it, is all the same to us";[35] if he failed to exercise his power and stop the killings, even out of fear, then he was responsible. But his role was more positive. According to his officials, he gave the orders. Felipe Arana, minister of Rosas and deputy governor during the terror of 1840–1842, disclaimed all responsibility for the decisions of that time: "Rosas, from Santos Lugares, issued the orders for those assassinations, without any participation at all by me or by the police or by the agents themselves." The chief of police, Bernardo Victorica, also denied responsibility and any duty to investigate. The reason he gave was that he knew that "the highest authority was aware of all those crimes and I was confirmed in this conviction because the government did not give me any warning"—until the decree stopping the terror, when he was blamed for lack of vigilance. No doubt testimony of this kind was suspect, for they were all trying to save their own skins during

Rosas's trial. This motive hardly applied, however, to Cuitiño, as he was unrepentant and prepared to go down fighting. Cuitiño declared to the court that the order to cut the throats of Colonel Francisco Lynch, Oliden, Máson, and the others "was received by Parra directly from Governor Rosas verbally" and that Parra reported directly to Rosas afterward at Government House; and in his own prison, Cuitiño had shot and cut the throats of detainees on the order of the government.[36] His testimony was probably true.

One way or another, Rosas obtained unqualified obedience. He destroyed anarchy, but he created a great fear. He wore down the opposition by irresistible force. After two memorable decades, he was still there, irremovable and apparently impervious not only to internal threat but also to foreign intervention.

7

HOPES AND FEARS

American Hero

Rosas could not apply terror so easily in the interior of Argentina. There he had to proceed by stealth and diplomacy. In the north and west he cultivated friends and fought enemies. In the littoral he succeeded gradually in imposing allied, dependent, or weak governors. In Uruguay, success did not come so easily, for local caudillism was supported by émigré unitarians and foreign enemies. France instituted a naval blockade of Buenos Aires from 1838 to 1840, as has been seen, but fortunately for Rosas, it failed to synchronize with the unitarian army of General Lavalle. Although the unitarians were defeated in the western provinces, Uruguay proved to be a running sore. Rosas imposed a blockade on Montevideo in 1843, but his subsequent siege of the city lasted nine years. British intervention was now the complicating factor.

In the course of 1843, British naval forces broke the blockade, saved Montevideo, prolonged the war, and pinned down Rosas to a long and costly siege. In addition to defending the independence of Uruguay, Britain also sought to open the rivers to free navigation. Anglo-French naval forces imposed a blockade on Buenos Aires from September 1845, and in November a joint expedition forced its way up the River Paraná, convoying a merchant fleet to inaugurate direct trade to the interior. But the expedition encountered neither welcoming allies nor promising markets, and the blockade hit foreign trade rather than the local enemy. Argentina's simple export economy made it virtually invulnerable to outside pressure. It could always revert to subsistence and sit it out, waiting for pent-up trade to resume while its cattle resources accumulated and no one starved.

As for the British, they simply blockaded their own trade. Rosas resisted the British without molesting their subjects. In fact, the British enjoyed a particular advantage from their treaty status, which gave them exemption from military service, forced loans, and live-stock requisitions. Assisted by the low price of land and, in a time of political tension, by the absence of competition from nationals, they bought their way into the rural sector. In the 1840s, they advanced rapidly in the sheep industry, acquiring land and flocks and further-ing the improvement of creole sheep by crossing them with merino imports.

Rosas was not alarmed by British penetration of the Argentine economy, seeing it as a natural process and mutual benefit. He could afford to be magnanimous, as he undoubtedly earned great credit at home from resisting French and British naval intervention in the Río de la Plata. His defiance, determination, and ultimate survival placed him among the nation's heroes and made a patriot for pos-terity. Argentina rallied round Rosas. The House of Representatives lauded him for giving the foreigners a lesson and teaching them to keep to commerce. Lorenzo Torres, a rosista nationalist, spoke for patricians and populace alike when he denounced the intervention as "a war of vandalism in which the principal role has been played by foreign swine."[1] The British themselves admitted that Rosas had improved his position. The dictator also received accolades, if little practical assistance, from other South American nations for his resistance to the imperial giants, and even Andrés Bello was moved to commend him for "conduct in the great American question which places him in my opinion in the leading ranks of the great men of America."[2] Americanism of this kind was not a feature of Argentine nationalism, whose day had yet to come. But it served some of Rosas's propaganda purposes. When the emergency was over and the British returned to seek peace and trade, they found the regime stronger than ever, the economy improving, and a golden age beginning. Were the signs sure?

Zenith

Rosas ruled according to fixed objectives and unyielding principles. But he responded to circumstances and the mood of the times. The mid-1840s were years of calm and stability, the great danger was over, and the regime became, if not benign, at least conciliatory. The Anglo-French blockade, it is true, tested Rosas and strained the economy, but it did not damage his reputation and was not accompanied by internal dissent. The terror of 1840–1842, therefore, was not repeated, and Rosas retained control without recourse to violence. Official propaganda was still extravagant, and the antiunitarian slogans were no less savage; but their application was no longer ferocious, and factionalism diminished. If the government remained the same and normal political life was still proscribed, the atmosphere was more relaxed, the regime more temperate, society less tormented.

The diarist Beruti dated the change from 1844, a year of peace and quiet: "There have been no outrages, confiscations, or throat-cuttings, and no one has been persecuted; God willing, may we thus continue from now on, until the general peace and constitution of the republic, which is what we all desire."[3] Two years later (June 1, 1846) he reported the demise of the mazorca and the dispersion of its members to the militia. In 1840, Rosas had declared implacable war on the unitarians and organized a thorough confiscation of their property. But from 1845 confiscated property was increasingly returned to its owners. Many rosistas, of course, had permanently profited from the confiscations, and their gains were not disturbed. But the government appeared anxious to liquidate the past and to welcome the restored proprietors back into the fold.

The trend continued. In 1848 the regime reached the peak of its power and repute. The country was united and strong at home and abroad. Rosas had impressed his character on every aspect of government and every sector of life down to the smallest detail of dress and behavior. He was obeyed, if not liked, in Buenos Aires and beyond. He had tamed the provincial caudillos and persuaded the provinces by terror or by interest that the hegemony of Buenos Aires was a reasonable price to pay for federal peace and order. He had successfully combated intervention by Britain and France and had earned some respect in the Americas for his achievement. Peace and security encouraged immigration and improved the labor supply. Political émigrés continued to return, and many found that it was still not too late to reclaim their lands and property.

There is also an immense influx of emigrants both of that class who arrive on these shores for the first time from foreign countries, and also of natives who have been long absent from political motives. Considerable numbers come to settle here from the town of Montevideo, and amongst them a great many who have borne arms during the late events. No inquiries however are made, and no one is molested for what may have taken place elsewhere. The returned refugees are also treated with every consideration, and the sequestration of their property is very frequently taken off on proper application being made to the Government.[4]

According to Saldías, after the repression and bloodshed committed by both sides, "the country in general began to enjoy a certain liberalism."[5] But these developments were not signs of liberalism; they meant rather that some émigrés, worn out by the length of their exile and the durability of the regime, lost all hope of change and were ready to return on the dictator's terms. The assassinations ceased, conciliation took the place of hatred, but the system remained otherwise the same. Behind the bland exterior, an iron resolve survived. It was in 1848 that Camila O'Gorman and her lover were executed. And it was at this time that the British minister reported the relentless insistence on outward conformity, which was the hallmark of the regime: "Every citizen of the Argentine Confederation in Buenos Ayres is obliged to wear a species of uniform, which is the distinctive mark of federalism. His waistcoat must be red, he must wear a red ribbon round his hat, and at his button hole another red ribbon bearing an inscription of 'Life to the Argentine Confederation' and 'Death to the Savage Unitarians.' The women are likewise bound to wear a knot of red ribbon in the hair."[6]

Rosas now had his principal residence at Palermo, whose buildings and parks were more or less complete and where a staff of 300 ranging from officials and secretaries to servants, overseers, and peons served the dictator. More than one English visitor remarked on his pastoral style: "In private life Rosas appears good natured. . . . He is hale looking, and vigorous in personal appearance, being more like a good looking English farmer than a Spanish general. His daughter is his real minister and secretary, and through her it is easy to convey any communication that it may be wished to make. She is amiable, apparently kind hearted and affectionate. Her manners and appearance are graceful, though she is no longer pretty. Her adoration for her father amounts to passion."[7]

William MacCann visited Rosas by invitation at this time and walked with him in the grounds under the shade of willow trees: "His handsome ruddy countenance, and portly aspect . . . gave him the appearance of an English country gentleman. He is in height about five feet ten inches, and his age is now fifty-nine years." At the time of MacCann's visit, Rosas was fifty-five, and as usual he was affable to his guests: "The address of General Rosas was so easy and familiar, that he at once made his visitors feel perfectly at their ease. . . . The most prejudiced stranger, upon leaving his presence, must have felt that intercourse with such a man was unrestrained and agreeable."[8] In less guarded moments, Rosas left a different impression; critics such as Sarmiento noted his liking for obscene stories and jokes, foul language, and gross physical clowning. But everyone agreed that his application to work was extraordinary.

In residence at Palermo surrounded by his staff, Rosas placed himself at a distance from his ministers; he no longer saw Arana and communicated with him only in the most formal manner. Ministers sent him the files of government business, and Rosas replied in writing. His secretaries worked nonstop in twelve-hour shifts. Interviews and business with his officials were conducted by Rosas striding up and down his long reception room, his secretaries scurrying after him and turning about in line at the end of the room. In effect, Rosas reduced the system of government to two sectors, his private office, which exercised real power, and the ministries, whose function was more formal. Henry Southern reported: "Administration is chiefly carried on by the Police, which is another branch of his private Government, and he has another branch of military private Secretaries at his Head Quarters which are about 12 miles from the town and which is the centre of all business relative to the Provinces. The Ministers are kept as ignorant of what is taking place as is possible consistent with a scrupulous observance of all official forms."[9]

This was personal government of the crudest kind; all policy decisions and most executive ones were made by Rosas, and no attempt was made to organize the delegation of administrative powers and functions. The only exception was the work done by his daughter, Manuelita, whom Southern described as "Rosas's redeeming Angel." She acted as a kind of filter through whom was transmitted business of an extrajudicial character, including petitions for clemency in sentences of confiscation, banishment, and even death. Otherwise the dictator took the whole weight of administrative detail indiscriminately upon himself: "He is constantly occupied in solitary study, thought and the labor of business, and accepts no aid save that of mechanical assistants."[10] According to Saldías, the task became too much for him: "The year 1848 was when his intellectual decline began," a process that could be seen in his vacillation, obsessions, eccentric behavior, and singular routine and in sudden outbursts of rage over trivial things. Southern thought there might be a touch of madness in his behavior: "He says himself that there is not a member of his family who is not *maniatico:* he is even something more. His aberrations I think at a times amount to something like flitting touches of madness: at all events he is in the highest degree, capricious and crotchety— slow to listen or rather to understand reasoning, and perhaps the most obstinate and bull-headed individual in existence."[11] One of his obsessions was crime and its authors.

In 1851, when external pressures on the regime built up once more, Rosas became concerned over law and order, remembering, perhaps, that combination of foreign attack and internal subversion that had so threatened him in 1840–1842. He became preoccupied with details of criminal behavior, urging the justices of the peace to greater efforts. He ordered them, for example: "In future each and every prisoner whom you send to these general headquarters must be interrogated to ascertain whether they frequently get drunk, whether they drink little or much, if they take bad or good drink, and if they are likely to fight or commit other acts of disorder through drink, and all of this you must note in the classifications which you send with them according to the enclosed model."[12] Police records gave an impression of a rise in crime rate—an increase in sexual crimes, street attacks, robbery with violence, forging of money, and desertions from the army. In the first half of 1851 a number of criminals were executed, not, as Rosas explained to Southern, "with the view of punishing the culprit, and scarcely in that of deterring other criminals, but simply to prevent them from again inflicting injury on society."[13]

Rosas himself believed that his regime had now achieved a balance between conservatism and moderation, and he proudly declared to the House of Representatives: "The timely repressive measures have produced indescribable benefits, and I have laboured incessantly in the scrupulous protection of all rights, properties, interests, public and private, national and foreign, and in acts of clemency. This harmony between conservative aims and moderate methods, in times of extraordinary political upheaval, have produced results on which I do not need to elaborate."[14]

Foreign observers, too, had this impression. Henry Southern, admittedly sympathetic to the regime, thought that the achievements of Rosas were now recognized: "Now that his sway is undisputed, and for the moment indisputable, it is seen that though sanguinary punishments cost him nothing, still he takes no pleasure in them, and that now that the time of struggle and danger is passed, the many eminent and valuable qualities which distinguish General Rosas become every day more conspicuous." And even at the end, on the eve of the last battle, he was telling foreigners of his dreams of a better future, as Robert Gore, the British chargé d'affairs, reported: "I have no doubt in my own mind that should General Rosas triumph he will pursue in a short time a very different system, and one which will develop the great riches of this magnificent country, ensure the rigid execution of the law and advance by education and otherwise, civilization and industry."[15]

Present Fears, Future Prospects

There was an inherent flaw in rosismo even at the height of its success. How could its stability be prolonged, its continuity ensured? Personal monarchy perpetuated itself by hereditary succession. A caudillo, however, could not even appoint a successor, much less hand over to an heir; indeed, the one thing he could not dictate was an orderly transfer of power. A personal regime of this kind could not normally guarantee its own survival or provide for the permanence of its policies. Brought to power by violence, or threat of violence, a caudillo could perish in the same way, and the system for which he stood could be extinguished by that of a rival. In addition to his real power, Rosas possessed a formal legitimacy, and to this he clung; in fact, he found it difficult to relinquish.

The House of Representatives had elected Rosas governor of

Buenos Aires with absolute power on December 6, 1829, and by the
law of August 2, 1830, he was authorized "extraordinary powers in
all their entirety, to be used according to the dictates of his own
knowledge and conscience."[16] At the end of 1832, he did not accept
reelection to another term of office, for the House was loath to
renew these powers. In 1835, however, he accepted appointment
once more when he was granted the *suma del poder,* that is, total
powers, to be used according to his knowledge and conscience. In
1840, he did not accept reelection, and the deputies found a saving
formula, the prorogation of his term of office, which he did not
seem to mind. At the beginning of 1842, protesting poor health, he
again requested the House of Representatives to find a successor;
again they did not do so, and again he continued to govern. The
same thing happened in 1843. In 1844, he was still "sacrificing his
health," and the House was still protesting its loyalty. During the
blockade of Montevideo and the Anglo-French intervention, Rosas
seemed especially indispensable. In 1845, he was reelected by unanimous vote of the House. In 1846, he again asked to be relieved
because his health was broken, and equally predictably the House
reelected him. The same routine, and almost the same words, were
adopted in 1847 and in 1848. Thus the play continued, and the
governorship of Rosas reached the year 1849.

Toward the end of 1849, Rosas seemed more determined than
usual to retire, showing perhaps genuine signs of fatigue, a sense that
things were slipping away, and an anxiety to relinquish the cares of
office. His main task, it could be argued, was now over. The country was at peace, law and order were secure, enemies were van-
quished, and prosperity was on the horizon. The reason he gave was
his exhaustion in the service of his country, the need to retire to private life and to make way for someone vigorous "who with more
determination and force of opinion may succeed to the office without delay."[17] His plea could also be interpreted as a means of obtaining a pseudoplebiscite, as encouraging the people to press for his
continuation in office. The agents of rosismo, not least the legislature itself, organized a clamorous campaign of demonstrations and
petitions, simulating public pressure from all sides. A mass petition
was presented to the House on October 18. Even the British merchant community joined in, requesting Southern to support the
movement for Rosas. The campaign came to a close at the end of the

year in an orgy of adulation. The House confirmed Rosas in
absolute power, limited only by his own will, declaring, "The world
knows that General Rosas and the Argentine Confederation are
today inseparable names. Remove the one and you lose the other."[18]

   There was, of course, a real obstacle to Rosas's retirement. Who
would succeed him? By a process of conformism, exclusion, and persecution, Rosas had removed all political talent and all possible
rivals. Politics were reduced to rosismo, and rosismo without Rosas
was unthinkable. The whole elaborate system of patronage
depended on him: he was the ultimate patrón, and his clients
became more anxious at each hint of resignation. No doubt some of
the rumors of administrative corruption, especially those circulating
among émigré groups in Montevideo that spoke of "immorality and
corruption in all branches of the administration" and "the arbitrari-
ness of the mandarins," were exaggerated for purposes of propaganda.[19] But there appears to have been a real decline, not merely
one of efficiency but one of morale and integrity. Many officers and
bureaucrats were making money out of the state, extending their
property, engaging in contraband, even trading with the enemy in
Montevideo. A government office was regarded as a private business,
and political slogans became meaningless: "He is surrounded by savage unitarians," complained Vicente González.[20] Rosas was now carrying the whole state: "The whole weight of the administration,"
reported Pedro de Angelis, "in details great and small, rests upon his
shoulders and what is more on his responsibility. The faults of officials, the abuses they commit, even their lack of education, all are
blamed on the government and attributed to his negligence and
even to his connivance."[21] Who could take over this responsibility?

   On December 27, 1849, Rosas continued his yearly practice of
presenting an annual message to the House of Representatives.
These policy reports became longer each year, though their value to
the historian does not increase with their prolixity. This time the
report was 453 pages long, and Rosas announced that three sessions
would be needed to read it; so the first three days of January were
allotted. The secretary of the House began reading on January 1 but
had only reached page 49 when the session concluded and the
drooping deputies made their exit. On the second day, he reached
only page 78, so two more days and a faster rate of reading were
required to complete the report and bring the tedium to a close. The

message was a verbose and complacent account of office and policy in which Rosas reached a familiar conclusion, that he had destroyed his health in the service of the republic and now wished to retire. Legally the governor's existing term of office ended in April 1850, and on March 7 the House unanimously elected Rosas governor and captain general. Members then had to persuade him to accept. "Every one of the representatives," they declared, "will always regard it as a mark of honor to have occupied a place in this Assembly during the time when General Rosas accomplished his great and admirable achievements and brought the Republic to its present state of prosperity."[22] Henry Southern observed Rosas going through paroxysms of frustration over his failure to resign: "Rosas himself I really believe is sometimes his own dupe and for the moment often identifies himself with the part he is playing. I apprehend that there is something unsound in the brain and though there is a constant method in his madness, still it must be hallucination. A few evenings ago when speaking of the cruelty of his fellow countrymen in forcing him to remain the supreme power in this part of the world his tone of lamentation and distress would have melted any heart not steeled by incredulity."[23]

At the beginning of October there was another request to Rosas to remain in office. He did not reply until December 13, 1850, when, in another long and rambling message, he reaffirmed his determination not to continue. These constant resignations puzzled Southern, especially as he could see no alternative to Rosas and no other barrier to anarchy; but, he asked, why should one judge the motives of "a man who has discovered the means of governing one of the most turbulent and restless people in the world?"[24] The fact was that while the House of Representatives and the governor went through the motions of election and refusal, Rosas continued to govern.

Having come to dominate Buenos Aires, Rosas now wished to confirm his sovereignty and strengthen his support in the provinces, but not through a constitutional settlement. The only existing constitutional provision was the Treaty of the Littoral of 1831, which left the national organization to a congress to be convened by agreement of the provinces. But Rosas preferred other means, a direct appeal to the provinces. When in 1849 he refused reelection, one of the reasons he gave was that "his reputation in the Province and the

Republic has naturally declined." This view was transmitted to the provinces, and the rosista political machines moved into action, as was intended, in order to prove it wrong. Across the land, governors and assemblies took the hint and competed with each other in political homage, applauding Rosas and beseeching him to continue. Santa Fe, Catamarca, Córdoba, San Juan, Tucumán, Salta, San Luis, Mendoza, Santiago del Estero, Corrientes, all sent their support. From Entre Ríos, Urquiza claimed for himself and his province "the high honor of always fighting in the vanguard against the rebel band of savage unitarians" and lent his adherence to "your great mission to save the fatherland and open the way to a new future."[25] Some provinces declared they wanted Rosas as governor; others, such as Salta, called him supreme head of the confederation; others assigned him the *suma del poder;* and one province proclaimed him president of the republic.

Rosas himself had already begun, from at least 1848, to use grander titles of a more national kind, though not defined by any law, such as *gobierno de la confederación, gobierno general, jefe supremo de la nación.* As a result of the campaign in the provinces, he now called himself *jefe supremo de la confederación Argentina.* In his message of 1850, he spoke of the governors and peoples of the provinces "who obey and respect the orders of the supreme head of the state" and of "Argentine government which speaks to its legislative body," thus claiming a national character for his government.[26] To some extent this statement reflected his real power and influence, but it did not mean that a national state existed or that Buenos Aires possessed the machinery of government to sustain one. To the very end, Rosas set himself against a constitutional organization of Argentina and stood firm for an undefined confederation in which Buenos Aires exercised de facto hegemony over a cluster of satellites. As he later explained, he remained opposed to a constitution on the grounds that "the habits of anarchy could not be changed in a day" and that a constitution could not create order, only reflect it. His view of government never faltered: "For me the ideal of happy government would be a paternal autocracy."[27]

The year 1851 opened full of uncertainty. The supreme head wanted to step down, or said he did. No one offered to come forward, or was allowed to. And the regime itself was suddenly challenged. There were rumors that Urquiza was organizing opposition in the littoral and talking of a constitution. An article in the Entre Ríos periodical *La Regeneración* (January 5) under the heading "El año 1851" declared that this would be known as "the Year of Organization." Rosas could not ignore the defiance. On March 15, 1851, the *Gaceta Mercantil* carried without explanation the celebrated letter of Rosas to Quiroga written at the Hacienda de Figueroa on December 20, 1834, in which he explained his conviction that it was not appropriate to impose a national constitution or call a general congress. And in April, in the *Archivo Americano,* the Entre Ríos article was reproduced and criticized as anarchy: "To organize the country is to disturb it."

While the provinces of the interior proclaimed their support for the supreme head of the confederation, elsewhere signs of disaffection appeared. There were three particular foci of criticism: the émigrés were still unreconciled; the economy gave cause for concern even within Buenos Aires; and the littoral now utterly rejected the economic policies of Rosas.

Encirclement

The political émigrés remained on their guard in the 1840s, unconvinced by the superficial moderation of the regime and rejecting the overtures of the dictator. Yet they too were affected by the circumstances of the time. The Young Generation was now more mellow. Émigré writings began to show a greater awareness of the achievements of Rosas, an appreciation of his particular talents, and concern for the future reconciliation of all Argentines. Even Sarmiento, one of the least yielding of liberals, was forced to give Rosas his due, and in 1844, he wrote a frank assessment of him, seeking to understand, the better to condemn:

> No one knows more shrewdly than General Rosas the social situation of the peoples who surround him. His long tenure of government, and the sharp and penetrating intelligence with which nature has, unfortunately, endowed him and which only mean party prejudice could deny, are sufficient to make him well informed of these things. . . .
> Raised to command of his country by a general insurrection of the masses; sustained in office by the power provided by this insurrection; master of this sector and connoisseur of its strength and instincts; conqueror, if not in battle at least by politics and achievements, of the educated and Europeanised part of the Argentine people; he has come to

have a complete understanding of the state of society in South America and always knows exactly how to touch the right social chords and to produce the sounds which he wants.

The fact is that today he certainly constitutes the premier military power of this continent; at least we are not aware of any other government in recent years which has had 12,000 veterans in the field and not less than 4,000 in reserve, as he has. General Rosas has never appeared on a field of battle, but he assumes the role of conqueror of the Republic of Uruguay; he will do the same in the case of Paraguay; and in time he will play the part of protector of the province of Rio Grande against the Empire of Brazil.[28]

A year later, in 1845, Sarmiento introduced in the final part of *Facundo* a program of national reconstruction that stood in contrast to the intransigence of the earlier chapters. People were not naturally criminals and murderers, he argued; it depended on the circumstances presented to them. A future Argentina, therefore, would have a place for honorable supporters of Rosas; even mazorqueros would not be excluded, for among them there were hidden virtues.[29]

Alberdi, too, attempted to understand the reasons for Rosas's political durability. His cool appraisal of Argentina thirty-seven years after the May Revolution (published as a pamphlet on May 25, 1847), although written from an overtly anti-Rosas standpoint, scandalized many exiles by its complacent view of the current situation. He saw the regime as an inevitable product of time and place. "Wherever there are Spanish republics, created from former colonies, there you will have dictators." This did not mean that Rosas was a mere tyrant. If he wielded a rod of iron, he also possessed political talent, and he had won such a reputation that he was better known in the world than Simón Bolívar and George Washington. He represented the typical qualities of Argentina. "As all outstanding men, the extraordinary development of his character reflects that of the society to which he belongs. Rosas and the Argentine Republic are mutually dependent things; he is what he is because he is Argentine; his rise supposes that of his country." He had many achievements to his credit: he had repelled Britain and France, created a powerful state, and established peace. As for the federal-unitarian conflict, it was not the responsibility of one side alone. "The federal party supported the tyranny; the unitarian league supported the foreigners. Both did wrong." Rivadavia may have proclaimed unity, but Rosas achieved it. "The unitarians have lost, but unity has triumphed. The federalists have won, but the federation has succumbed." Rosas, moreover, had promoted the lower classes to power and had helped to educate them in government and politics. Nevertheless, concluded Alberdi, Rosas had wasted his opportunities; in the final analysis, he failed because he had not given Argentina a constitution:

> There is no written constitution in the Argentine Republic, nor are there individual laws of a fundamental character. The operation of those which used to exist in Buenos Aires is suspended, while General Rosas retains indefinitely the *suma del poder público*. . . . He is a dictator, a leader invested with despotic and arbitrary powers, in the exercise of which there is no counterweight. . . . To live in Buenos Aires is to live under the regime of a military dictatorship. Extol the moderation of that power if you wish, in which case it will be a worthy dictatorship. But in our time ideas have reached a point where mixed constitutions have more appeal than benevolent dictatorships.[30]

Rosas liked Alberdi's pamphlet and invited the author to return. But Alberdi did not wish to be co-opted into the regime anymore than he intended to shock his fellow exiles in Chile and Montevideo. The work should be read in the context in which it was written, expressing as it did a fierce patriotism and sense of national identity so necessary to the exile that it embraced even the dictatorship in its search for an Argentine consensus and offered even Rosas the collaboration of the exiles in the task of reconciliation. It was written, moreover, before a foreign audience, among whom Alberdi did not wish to disparage his country.

The intellectual opposition to Rosas, therefore, endured the frustration of exile and resisted truce with the regime. Equally, however, Rosas survived opposition. A political campaign could not defeat the dictatorship without the support of an interest group and the backing of a military base. Were there any signs of weakness in the economic structure, or of weakening in economic support?

The triumphant years of Rosas seemed to demonstrate that he could guarantee peace for Buenos Aires and prosperity for its people, even if it was at the expense of other parts of the Río de la Plata. From 1848 to 1851, Buenos Aires was in a position to export its produce in relatively normal conditions, to receive increased imports, and to reexport some to the provinces. The end of the blockade brought not only much-needed imports but also new immigrants, who swelled the ranks of producers and consumers. The building industry went back to work, and Buenos Aires renewed its growth. Urban development was accompanied by other benefits. The government obtained an increase in income and customs revenue. Cheap consumer goods gave an impression of improved living standards among the mass of the people, and for the upper classes there were more European clothes, hats, shoes, and books in the shops. In March 1849 there were 189 vessels in the port, of which 35 were British. In other ways, too, British influence reasserted itself. Sporting people went to the races run according to Newmarket rules; others attended meetings of the Buenos Aires Total Abstinence and Beneficial Society. Although these last years of the Rosas regime were not exactly in the style of a belle époque, they were probably its best.

Yet the economic structure was not as stable as it looked. The renewal of exports, sudden population growth, increased demand, and a severe drought caused a surge of inflation in 1850. Immigration hardly had time to solve the chronic labor shortage before manpower was further reduced by conscription for war and, in 1851, almost universal military service. Rosas could not leave well enough alone. The supposed guarantor of peace, he appeared too ready to start war. He still wanted to control Uruguay and recover Paraguay, if necessary by force. And the expenses supporting these ambitions were not the only strains on the economy.

Merchants, artisans, and farmers complained of the shortage of currency and the high price of money. Currency fluctuations indeed played havoc with economic transactions and with the fortunes of import-export houses. In late 1850, when war with Brazil seemed likely, the value of currency on October 11 fell from 62 to 85 pesos to the pound sterling, or about 37 percent. Once fear of war subsided, the value rose within a month to 60 pesos, or by 30 percent. Merchants had the greatest difficulty in obtaining funds from London, and the price of gold rose every day. Moreover, not only was the economy handicapped by a depreciated and inconvertible paper currency but even it was in short supply owing to the government's practice, especially in the war-crisis years of 1850–1852, of hoarding it for its own purposes. "The customs duties," reported the

British minister, "have given the government a very considerable surplus of revenue which is paid in paper; and this surplus is hoarded
by the Treasury. . . . The accumulation has now reached to that
excess that over one third of the only permitted circulating medium
is detained by the Government, with what object is unknown."[31]
The result was a rise in prices, and exporters who had seen sterling
fall 50 percent in two years could not pay the prices producers were
asking for their commodities. So trade stagnated and the vital export
flow was stemmed. There were, of course, other theories invoked to
explain the economic difficulties of 1851. The official version was
that the extraordinary postblockade influx of imports, beyond the
capacity of the market, and the prolonged drought, which reduced
production and therefore purchasing power, were the basic causes of
the trouble. The exiles attributed the economic problems to diminished consumption brought on by social and political repression.
Whatever the reason, the golden years soon ceased to glisten.

The Rosas system depended not only on repression but also on
the assurance of continued benefits to various sectors. The key to the
system lay in export capacity. Good export prices satisfied the
landowners and saladeristas, who were also virtually immune from
taxes. Ample government revenue enabled the regime to meet the
expenses of the large army, which was simultaneously an instrument
of the state and a major buyer in the internal market. Only an abundant and constant customs revenue could sustain such an allocation
of resources—one of the reasons Rosas could never agree to diminish the customs monopoly of Buenos Aires or relinquish his economic control in favor of the provinces. The whole system thus
rested on three bases—the hegemony of the landowners, the presence of the army, and the subordination of the provinces. And now
the supports themselves began to shift.

An economy of hides and salt beef could not generate growth. It
perpetuated a primitive technology and low level of employment,
and it depended on markets that were inherently stagnant. The
export of salt beef was confined to Brazil and Cuba, slave markets
that might survive the abolition of slavery but that would probably
not expand. The production of hides, especially following the great
land rush and estancia expansion of 1820–1840, exceeded the
demand of the British market. In the 1840s the European market for
hides provided an added outlet, but by then other areas of produc-

tion were competing with Buenos Aires, not least the saladeros of Río Grande do Sul. In compensation for these constraints, the Buenos Aires economy began to develop an alternative activity, sheep farming. The last decade of the Rosas regime saw many estancias, or parts of estancias, change from cattle to sheep, and raw wool began to improve its export performance. Appropriate labor was available, as Irish, Basque, and Galician immigrants took advantage of the peaceful conditions after the blockades. These developments indicated that rosismo could adjust to change and accommodate alternative economic activities, but they also had less favorable implications. Sheep farming involved social as well as agricultural change, introducing new settlers far removed in values and style from the rural barons and their hordes who had first ridden in support of Rosas. Sheep farmers, their partners, and shepherds were less ideologically committed to Rosas than the original cattle ranchers of the province; they were less militarized, less mobile, more domestic and "civilian," than the rosista estancieros of the past. These new values and orientations implied an erosion of the primitive social base of rosismo, rooted in the cattle estancia and the rural militia.

A further implication of economic change concerned the provinces. If Buenos Aires could develop a new agricultural sector, so could the other littoral provinces, whose land and resources were an extension of the pampas and similarly endowed. The livestock industry of the littoral, especially that of Entre Ríos and Corrientes, also underwent growth during these years; and in times of blockade, when the trade of Buenos Aires was bottled up, these provinces could enter into open, if unauthorized, competition. This competition was not yet serious economically, least of all in wool, but it had political significance. Before 1852, exports of salt beef from Entre Ríos were only 10 percent those of Buenos Aires. But the obstacles they encountered from the policy of Buenos Aires far outweighed the economic calculation. The so-called unification of Argentina by Rosas was a facade; it was rather the conquest of Argentina by Buenos Aires. Provincial economic interests eventually revolted against the domination of Buenos Aires, its control of customs, monopoly over federal revenues, and prohibition of free commerce. It was a unitarian Florencio Varela who forecast that the territories of the littoral would be the hidden reefs on which the dictatorship foundered and that the demand for free river navigation would unite them into a league to confront Rosas. "The littoral provinces of the Paraná, ruined by a continuous series of futile and useless wars, and impoverished by the economic isolation and tutelage to which they are subject, have more interest than any other people in the world in promoting such a league."[32]

8

EXIT AND EXILE

Rosas in His Bunker

The world outside might be hostile, but Rosas was still secure in his essential power base, the city and province of Buenos Aires. Here in his innermost fortress there was no loosening of control, no sign of opposition, no political change. The regime seemed as powerful as ever, destined to endure for many years to come and to yield at last the benefits it had always promised. As there was no way of undermining the dictatorship from within, it could be destroyed only by a shock from without. This was precisely where the threat originated, and ironically, Rosas himself helped to create it. He saw the danger, and his campaign to rally the provinces was serious enough. But it proved to be a useless charade: in the event the provinces would be either indifferent, impotent, or hostile. Provincial hostility on its own, however, was not enough, for the provinces did not have the military power to tip the balance against Buenos Aires. Any province taking the initiative would need the added weight of outside support. And this, too, Rosas helped to provoke.

In October 1850, Brazil broke off relations with Rosas, formed an alliance with Paraguay on December 24, and reached an understanding with Entre Ríos early in 1851. In every case the independence of Uruguay was invoked as a primary objective of the allies. Entre Ríos declared war on Rosas in May 1851, and Corrientes did likewise. A formal league among Brazil, Entre Ríos, and Uruguay was established on May 29, 1851; it was later expanded to include Corrientes and Paraguay, the object being to overthrow the common enemy, Rosas. Operations began in Uruguay with such success that Oribe surrendered on October 8. The day of reckoning for Rosas was coming close. How can we account for this unprecedented alliance?

Once the Anglo-French intervention was formally ended by treaties with Britain (1849) and France (1850), Buenos Aires was free to confront Brazil. Both were already involved in the Guerra Grande, the prolonged civil war in Uruguay between rival caudillos and opposing factions. Rosas supported Oribe, encamped outside the capital, and Brazil supported the government of Montevideo, besieged within. Brazil believed it had to sustain Montevideo and Paraguay in order to keep Rosas and his satellites from her southern frontier. She decided, therefore, to favor the unitarian and antirosista forces in Montevideo and to aid the cause of Uruguayan independence, though in return for heavy concessions and while pursuing an expansionism of her own. Brazil was concerned for the security of Río Grande do Sul not simply as its southernmost province but also as a moving economic frontier; it also wanted the free navigation of the Paraná and an independent and friendly Paraguay.

Rosas saw these ambitions as Brazilian imperialism in the Río de la Plata. In his view, Rio Grande do Sul was simply a base for Brazilian penetration southward, an independent Paraguay was no more than a satellite of Brazil, and freedom of navigation amounted to expansion of Brazilian naval power. To prevent Brazil leapfrogging over her satellites into the Río de la Plata, Rosas had to strengthen his northern front and prevent the governments of Uruguay and Paraguay from falling into the power orbit of Brazil and becoming channels of further imperial expansion. Rosas had never recognized Paraguay as an independent nation. He still called it the *provincia del Paraguay* and sought its "recovery," aiming to extend the frontiers of the confederation to those of the old Spanish viceroyalty. Uruguay was an exception because its independence had been secured by treaty and its conquest would be extremely difficult. So it was improbable that Rosas wished to destroy the independence of Uruguay; it suited him better to reduce it to satellite status, the natural destiny of a weaker neighbor.

The defense of the northeastern front had not been neglected. To contain the Paraguayans, who were not expected to fight far from home, the militia of Corrientes and a river squadron were regarded as sufficient. The major effort was reserved for the security of the littoral against Brazil. Here, Rosas had the *ejército de operaciones* under

Urquiza, 10,000 strong, which he reinforced with arms and troops from March 1850. He also had the *ejército aliado* of Manuel Oribe, another veteran force of 10,000, whose role was to maintain the siege of Montevideo and guard the security of the Banda Oriental. Finally, he had the cavalry of Mansilla and other troops, some 20,000 between Santos Lugares and Palermo, as a reserve army and defense force. He was aware of his deficiencies in naval power, and in 1851, he took delivery of two warships purchased in Trieste. Apparently, therefore, Rosas had a powerful army of veteran Argentine troops led by experienced officers and commanded by the best general in Argentina, Urquiza. But what should have been his greatest strength turned into a fatal weakness. Rosas had committed the ultimate defense of Buenos Aires and his regime to generals who were basically provincial caudillos and had stationed his best troops and arms in the littoral because he identified Brazil as the principal threat to his security, and indeed, the littoral was where his most dangerous opponents and their allies were to emerge. But this strategy meant that these caudillo generals and their forces—in effect, Rosas's best armies—were vulnerable to Brazil, either through defection or defeat. The stronger Rosas became, the more vulnerable he was.

In the course of 1850, Rosas increased his military preparations. From March, these were directed overtly against Paraguay to counter its incursions into Misiones, but the more important objective was a war with Brazil. On October 2–3 the House of Representatives whipped itself into a frenzy of war fever, deputies striving to outdo each other in hostility toward Brazil. A mob went rampaging through the streets, shouting for war. Henry Southern was convinced, however, that beneath this outward enthusiasm there was popular hostility toward a war policy because of the material sacrifices involved: "The evils of war are no where felt more cruelly than in these provinces, where the sacrifices of both persons and property are made for the support of it in the most painful form, and as the community is wholly agricultural and commercial, and as the native products of every kind are almost wholly intended for exportation, war strikes at the very root of the well being of nearly every individual in the country, whether native or foreign."[1]

The rosista point of view was summed up by the priest Esteban Moreno, who declared, "The Empire [of Brazil] is our natural enemy";[2] he called for immediate war. Yet many of Rosas's defense measures further dissipated his forces and placed him at risk. In June, he acquired a squadron of riverboats, including steamers, and with these he sent Urquiza reinforcements and further supplies of artillery and munitions. While Rosas gave hostages to fortune, his enemies were preparing the coalition against him. On December 24, 1850, an alliance of Brazil and Paraguay was signed to defend the independence of each and to secure the free navigation of the rivers Paraguay and Plata "as far as their mouth." This was only the beginning. A more acute threat would be presented by an alliance between Entre Ríos and Brazil.

Entre Ríos was the greatest danger to Rosas, for it had the interests, the resources, and the leader to defy him. Inland navigation for hundreds of miles enabled shipping to penetrate into the heart of the country to pick up produce, and in Paraná, primitive though it was, the province had a river port that could export successfully and, given favorable conditions, compete with Buenos Aires. The resource base was livestock, estancias, and saladeros with an arable sector protected by high tariffs against imports from other provinces. It was the Anglo-French blockade of Buenos Aires that provided the most effective stimulus to Entre Ríos, enabling it to develop an active trade from its own ports or from Rosario direct to Montevideo and from there to Europe and the United States; thus, its export trade escaped the tutelage of Buenos Aires, and it also diverted imports from Montevideo. After the blockade, exporters and shippers from Entre Ríos openly ignored the fiscal and commercial constraints reaffirmed by Rosas. The time had come for Entre Ríos to reconsider its situation—to reject porteño control of customs and terminate the policy of a single port of entry and exit.

Meanwhile, the political and military career of Justo José de Urquiza was providing the means and the resources for implementing this decision. Urquiza, like Rosas, was a rural caudillo, the owner of vast estates, the ruler of a personal fiefdom several hundred square miles in extent with tens of thousands of cattle and sheep and four saladeros. He made a fortune in the 1840s as a supplier to besieged Montevideo, an importer of manufactured goods, and an exporter of gold to Europe. His private ambitions combined easily with provincial interests, and as a politician he was willing to supplant Rosas and initiate a constitutional reorganization of Argentina. He displayed, moreover, greater deference to education, culture, and freedom than his rival, and he had a superior reputation with the émigré intellectuals in Montevideo. In the person of Urquiza, therefore, the various strands of opposition came together, and he placed himself at the head of provincial interests, liberal exiles, and Uruguayan patriots in an alliance that needed only the backing of Brazil to tip the balance against Rosas.

Urquiza declared open rebellion against Rosas in his *pronunciamiento* of May 1, 1851. In this declaration, he assumed the powers of a head of a sovereign state, "qualified to deal directly with governments in the rest of the world."[3] The effect was that Rosas's *ejército de operaciones* and its commander withdrew from the confederation to ally with Brazil in a war against Rosas. With an army of only 15,000, Urquiza could not defeat Rosas, who still had 25,000 troops at his disposal; Urquiza needed Brazil, which had a large army stationed in Río Grande do Sul and whose warships were already protecting the trade of Entre Ríos. The alliance was formalized on May 29, 1851, when a treaty between Brazil, Entre Ríos, and Montevideo was concluded to make war on Oribe and Rosas. From other provinces, however, Urquiza received no support. The governors, rosistas all, declared themselves unanimously against Urquiza and rejected his invitation to rebel.

The news of Urquiza's rebellion was published in Buenos Aires in the *Gaceta Mercantil* on May 20, 1851. There was a storm of protest against the "perfidious Empire," the "vile traitor sold to Brazilian gold," "the mad Urquiza." From now on Urquiza was officially designated "the mad traitor, the savage unitarian Urquiza," and thus he was named in all public statements and documents. In the military parade on July 9, despite torrential rain, Rosas marched at the head of the Palermo Division, shouting "Long live the Argentine Confederation!" and "Death to the mad traitor and savage unitarian Urquiza!" to demonstrate his resilience and rejection of the pronunciamiento. Then, after further mass demonstrations in his favor, he did what he was beseeched; he withdrew his resignation and agreed to continue in government. On September 15, 1851, a large attendance (forty deputies) in the House of Representatives and a crowd of people in the visitors' gallery heard Lorenzo Torres announce that to defeat Urquiza and his masters, the perfidious Brazilians, Rosas had decided to continue in office, even to jeopardize his "important health" in the struggle against the mad traitor.[4] Then the deputies threw themselves into an orgy of rosismo, their speeches becoming an anthology of contemporary political idiom in praise of Rosas and abuse of his enemies. These sentiments were repeated in streets, theaters, and demonstrations of all kinds; governors, provincial deputies, army officers, officials, magistrates, and clergy all declared their loyalty to Rosas and hatred of Urquiza and the Brazilians. In the event, the deputies were not at all conspicuous in the final battle, if they were even there.

Rosas began to take defense measures. One of the last laws sanctioned by the House of Representatives was that of September 20, 1851, which placed the suma del poder público and all the resources of Buenos Aires—the fortunes and lives of its inhabitants without limits or exceptions—at the disposal of Rosas to wage war against Urquiza. In September 1851, Rosas was not without troops and arms. In Buenos Aires and its environs, he had 12,000 men; in the Banda Oriental, he had 14,000 under Oribe. He desperately tried to recruit more to replace the lost army of Urquiza, once his pride, now the enemy. In recent years, he had supplied Urquiza not only with men but also with his best resources of horses, arms, and ammunition, all of which were difficult to replace. He bought abroad—rifles and artillery in Belgium, ships where he could. He formed new regiments at Santos Lugares, he supplemented the battalions that garrisoned the city, and he reinforced the Palermo Division, his own particular unit. He fortified various points on the Paraná to dispute the river passage of the Brazilian squadron.

Yet Rosas had no strategic plan. After a lifetime of command, he was now a servant of events, not their master. He still took no initiative against the Brazilians, although their vessels were moving freely in the Río de la Plata and operating unchallenged in the rivers Uruguay and Paraná. It was August 18, 1851, before he even declared war on Brazil. At Montevideo, Oribe had a good army, probably Rosas's best, with a backbone of 5,000 tough Argentine troops, veterans of many of the dictator's campaigns. But although this army was superior to that of Urquiza, it was not powerful enough to resist a double thrust from Urquiza and the Brazilians.

Urquiza's army invaded Uruguay on July 18–19, 1851. On September 4 a Brazilian army of 16,000 did likewise, and its mere

presence became sufficient reinforcement. Urquiza entered the
Banda Oriental not only with an army and an ally but also with a
policy of conciliation—"there are neither victors nor van-
quished"—which, with other inducements, won over a number of
Oribe's Uruguayan commanders and eventually Oribe himself.
Indeed, Oribe offered no resistance: he capitulated on October 8,
1851, "with discredit, if not dishonor," on the basis of political
amnesty and the independence of Uruguay.[5] He effectively betrayed
Rosas in accepting defeat at the hands of an inferior force and without putting up a fight. He also weakened his leader's resources. All
the arms and ammunition sent by Rosas to Oribe at the end of
1850, worth some 1.5 million pesos, fell into Urquiza's hands
together with the 5,000 veterans of the First Argentine Division.
These were basically loyal troops, but they needed orders, and in
the event, they had not been sent into action against Urquiza; they
were cornered and presented with a fait accompli. Now Rosas desperately wanted to get them back, the more so because the
Argentine troops in Urquiza's army, faced with the same dilemma,
had accepted the new command.

Rosas earnestly requested the British minister, Henry Southern,
to authorize the Royal Navy to transport the troops across the River
Plate and protect also the shipment of their arms, equipment,
artillery, and horses. Southern was sympathetic toward Rosas, whom
he regarded as the only man standing between Argentina and chaos,
and he preferred him to all his enemies, foreign and provincial. But
in this case there was nothing he could do. The British naval forces
in the river were bound to neutrality, and although they gave passage to a few Argentine officers, they could not evacuate an entire
division. So the First Division was lost to Rosas. As Urquiza boasted,
"All the personnel and material of the army of Buenos Aires are
incorporated into the liberating forces," though not, it must be
added, to the ultimate advantage of those forces. The "treachery" of
Oribe, inexplicable except as an expression of deep disillusion with
this endless and fruitless war, produced a sensation in Buenos Aires,
where Southern believed that a similar collapse could take place
through want of stomach for war: "The population were quite as
exhausted and wearied of war as in the Banda Oriental: their dispo-
sition would be, were they consulted, to make any sacrifice for
peace."[6]

Enemies and Allies

The march on Buenos Aires needed more careful preparation than the battle of the Banda Oriental. The treaty of November 21, 1851, between Brazil, Uruguay, and "the states of Entre Ríos and Corrientes" finalized the support that Urquiza wanted and that he regarded as the minimum necessary for making the decisive push against Rosas. "The Allied States solemnly declare that they do not seek to make war on the Argentine Confederation. . . . The sole object is to liberate the Argentine people from the oppression which they suffer under the tyrannical domination of the Governor Don Juan Manuel de Rosas." The war would be waged only by Entre Ríos and Corrientes, Brazil simply acting as an auxiliary. Brazil would station its principal army of 12,000 in a reserve position on the coast of Uruguay but would also attach 3,000 troops to Urquiza's army of 24,000 and provide a substantial quantity of artillery, arms and ammunition; naval support for the crossing of the Paraná; and a monthly subsidy to be repaid with 6 percent interest "by the government which will succeed general Rosas."[7] Paraguay joined the alliance on condition that the Argentine Confederation recognized its independence. Finally, in the course of November, Urquiza received political reinforcements when exiles from Chile, Sarmiento and Mitre among them, joined the allied army. Sarmiento had been convinced since 1848 that Urquiza would rise against Rosas and had offered his services since February 1851; but the political ideas of the two men were far apart, and their relations were never cordial.

The greatest liability assumed by Urquiza in the treaties of November 1851 was the obligation of Entre Ríos and Corrientes to grant free navigation of the Argentine rivers and to regulate this traffic with the allied states if a new central government did not do so. In the meantime, Urquiza depended on Brazilian naval power in Argentine waters and a Brazilian army on Argentine territory. Argentina, of course, was not fully a nation; nor had its inhabitants yet developed an overriding sense of national identity. In any case the allies and their theorists stoutly denied that they were deserting the cause of the nation. The policy of Rosas, even his resistance to foreign intervention, had never evoked a positive national response because it was seen essentially as a defense of provincial, not national, interests. Consequently, it was possible to enlist the foreigner to overthrow Rosas, a provincial governor, without affronting national susceptibilities. To oppose Rosas, to refuse to follow his Brazilian policy, to support his foreign enemies, was not to dismember Argentina or to offend Argentine nationality, for as Florencio Varela had long argued, Rosas's war "is not a national war" but a conflict of one part of Argentina against another.[8]

Urquiza's army embarked at Montevideo toward the end of October in three Brazilian vessels and was transported to Entre Ríos. From there it began its great campaign, crossing the Paraná unopposed on December 23–24, 1851, and thus winning its first victory. Pascual Echagüe, governor of Santa Fe and one of Rosas's staunchest supporters, having been denied reinforcements by his master to dispute the crossing of the Paraná and unable to count on the people of his province for military resistance, crumbled before Urquiza and took flight across the pampas to Buenos Aires. Now a number of regional commanders in Santa Fe, Rosario, and San Nicolás went over to the allies, hoping to keep their commands under a new regime. But San Nicolás was the last of these defections. From then on the "liberators" were received with general hostility; they obtained no information from the local population and no assistance. At the beginning of the campaign, therefore, what was the balance of advantage between Urquiza and Rosas?

From his headquarters at Diamante, Urquiza, who was now general in chief of the allied army, had issued a proclamation: "The campaign which we are about to begin is holy and glorious, because in it we are going to decide the fate of a great nation, which for twenty years has groaned under the heavy yoke of the tyranny of the Dictator of the Argentines, and to complete the great work of the social regeneration of the Republics of the Plate, in order to inaugurate the new era of civilisation, peace and liberty."[9] As the army set off on the long march to Buenos Aires, a gaucho army no less than that of Rosas, Sarmiento had his doubts about the level of civilization among the liberators.

Sarmiento was the only Argentine officer dressed as a European, looking rather incongruous in his frock coat and kepi. His choice of dress was a matter of principle, a protest against barbarism, against Rosas and the caudillos, a campaign for the uniform over the *chiripá,* for citizens over gauchos. "As long as we do not change the dress of the Argentine soldier," he said, "we are bound to have caudillos." But he was a strange sight among the gauchos, lances, and ponchos with his smart uniform and traveling printing press.

He acted as a combination of chronicler and publicity officer of the allied campaign, a role that was not entirely appreciated by the uncultivated Urquiza, who remarked that "for all the screaming of the press in Chile and elsewhere, it did not frighten Juan Manuel de Rosas, on the contrary he got stronger every day." Sarmiento was outraged. "Tyrants can only be overthrown by other tyrants," he had written in 1849, and he accepted Urquiza as the lesser evil. But he never forgot the insult. He was not alone in his alienation. The Brazilian contingent resented the attitude of the Argentines, which they thought was arrogant and condescending and neglectful of their welfare. Their commanding officer, Brigadier Márquez, complained to Sarmiento that Urquiza marginalized his unit, ignored him, and gave him no orders, no horses, no assistance of any kind. Sarmiento replied that Urquiza was "a poor peasant without education" and that the so-called Argentine army was nothing more than a *levée en masse* of country dwellers.[10]

Urquiza's army had other flaws. It was essentially a caudillo's army; it had no general staff, no orders of the day, no drill, no engineers, no commissariat, and no hospital. It relied on the Brazilians for river transport, and they at least supplied the advantage of naval power. Yet Urquiza approached Buenos Aires in a wide arc from the west, which isolated him for some time from his allies and bases and naval support but which he hoped gave him access to the resources of the pampas in cattle and water, placed him between Rosas and his allies in the interior, and brought him to a position where he could block a possible escape route to the south. Rosas failed to exploit Urquiza's weaknesses. He did not move to join forces with Santa Fe and dispute the crossing of the Paraná at Diamante. He did not trap Urquiza in the middle of the open pampas. On the contrary, he ordered his vanguard commanders, Pacheco and Hilario Lagos, to avoid action and withdraw to Puente de Márquez. The prescribed strategy was purely defensive and consisted in retreating before the enemy; stripping the countryside of cattle, horses, and supplies; and concentrating men and resources in Buenos Aires. Rosas's objective was to end the war in one big battle at the gates of the capital. This goal required abandoning the defense of the Paraná, forsaking his frontiers and territory, and leaving Urquiza's army free to move as it wished. Yet had he any alternative? He was now reluctant to entrust his officers with independent command too far from Buenos Aires, and recent experience did nothing to reassure him. Moreover, the Brazilians had an army across the river, and if Rosas moved out of the capital, they might move in, either by force or through the inertia of the inhabitants. Rosas had to remain in Buenos Aires; he had to guard against two armies, keep both guessing, and move quickly at the last minute against one. This extent of military imbalance had been imposed by foreign intervention.

What support did Rosas have at this, the most critical stage of his regime? In Buenos Aires itself the outward signs of popular allegiance were undiminished. On September 20, 1851, the House of Representatives appointed a commission to present to Rosas in person all the laws recently enacted confirming his powers in office and in war. A great demonstration was organized for Sunday, September 28. From early morning, people of all social classes flocked to Palermo on foot, by horse, and in carriages. The official procession began to form at 11 A.M., organized by the chief of police and his staff and including officials, justices of the peace, priests, military, representatives of parishes, and the deputies from the provinces. The column of riders and carriages moved off from the town center at 1:45 P.M. and made its way along the riverbank to Palermo with flags and banners waving, shouts resounding, and numbers increasing as the march proceeded. At Palermo the marchers merged with earlier arrivals, and they swarmed over the gardens and crowded into the corridors of the residence. After the ceremonies and speeches, Rosas moved among the multitude, talking and joking while people pressed around him, anxious to see and touch, until at 6 o'clock they began to move back to town. The chief of police estimated that over 300 carriages, 2,230 riders, and a crowd of 15,000 came out for Rosas on that memorable Sunday, an occasion that left a vivid impression on the minds of even less partial observers. These penultimate weeks of the regime sounded a triumphant note in defiance of the approaching storm. A series of extravagant events marked the enactment of the law of September 20, 1851, and gratitude to Rosas was expressed in salvos, fireworks, illuminations, demonstrations, parades, and theater shows.

Popular support of this kind was organized, not spontaneous, and the people were brought into the streets by magistrates and priests to raise morale and rally support. This organized effort itself was significant, for it indicated that the rosista political machine was still functioning and compliance was still the norm. But the element of manipulation was always paramount. If these demonstrations were taken at face value, Rosas was loved as well as feared. But in fact, it was terror that inspired obedience and dread that kept people in line. Henry Southern reported of these years, "Were Rosas obliged to retreat from Buenos Ayres tomorrow, he would be followed in his wanderings in the plains by every respectable man in the city and of course by the rabble who are his soldiers. These respectable men nearly all hate his rule, and still they would be found without exception by his side. Rosas says to his intimates, and I have it from one of them, 'Those who wish me well, will go with Headquarters; those who remain behind, will have their throats cut.' "[11] British observers, although generally sympathetic to the rule of Rosas, believed that most of the population of Buenos Aires preferred peace to war and would not fight a war of resistance. Southern thought that "the state of men's minds" was antiwar. And at the beginning of 1852, Robert Gore also inferred that the people were tired of war, that there was much disaffection in Buenos Aires, and that Rosas would probably not survive the year as leader: "There is no sympathy for Urquiza in Buenos Aires, but there is a very general desire for peace, to permit individuals to attend to their private affairs, which have owing to the war long remained in a neglected state; it is likewise feared, that should Rosas triumph the war will be prolonged ad infinitum, as he will after putting down Urquiza go to war with Paraguay and Brazil."[12] He concluded that the mass of the people lacked enthusiasm and would prefer that Urquiza be quietly permitted to overthrow Rosas.

In the countryside, support for Rosas was more spontaneous. As the army of Urquiza marched through the pampas and into the province of Buenos Aires, it had to contend not only with the suffocating heat, the untrodden and often burning terrain, and the shortage of food and water but also with the sullen hostility of the people, few and scattered but unmistakably rosista. The people of the plains passively resisted the liberators, refusing them information, contact, and supplies and remaining faithful to their caudillo.

According to César Díaz, commander of the Uruguayan Division, the allied army could not help but notice that "the spirit of the inhabitants of the countryside of Buenos Aires was completely favorable to Rosas," though this support was attributed to force: "It was obvious that the terror which this man instilled had become deeply rooted and that up to then no influence had weakened it." Even Urquiza was amazed and troubled to see "that a country so badly treated by the tyranny of that barbarian had rallied in mass to his support." Díaz further recorded that Urquiza "complained, and rightly, that he had not found in the province of Buenos Aires the slightest co-operation, the least sign of sympathy" and that he frankly admitted, "If it were not for the interest I have in promoting the organization of the Republic, I would have remained allied to Rosas, for I am convinced that he is a very popular man in this country." As for Díaz himself, he conceded that Rosas was popular; otherwise it would be difficult to explain why the population rejected the liberty offered to them: "I have a deep conviction, formed by the events which I have witnessed, that the prestige of his rule in 1852 was as great as or perhaps greater than it had been ten years before, and that the submission of the people and even their belief in his superior talent had never been withdrawn."[13]

There was, finally, support for Rosas even within the allied army. The Argentines in its ranks, those who had fought long and hard for the federal cause, or at least for Rosas, did not change their sympathies overnight, and although they obeyed Urquiza as commander in chief, they resented the proximity of former enemies and the alliance of foreign powers. According to General José María Francia, "We had contracted a serious pledge of honor, if our army were victorious in battle and General Rosas were taken prisoner, we did not intend to allow the slightest harm to come to him nor any humiliation at the hands of his enemies, and we would even seek to become his guard."[14] The hard core of rosista troops was to be found in the Argentine unit summarily transferred from the army of Oribe to that of Urquiza in October 1851. These men had been sent by Rosas to the Banda Oriental in 1837, when many of them were already veterans of the Indian wars. Fourteen years later they were still fighting in the siege of Montevideo, almost forgotten, without promotion or prospects but with a blind faith in Rosas and loyalty to his cause. They made an indelible impression on Sarmiento, who saw them as a monstrous embodiment of rosista barbarism; out of 414 soldiers and noncommissioned officers in the Aquino regiment, only seven could read and write, and many officers, too, were illiterate. Sarmiento left a vivid description of these terrible *tercios* of Rosas: clothed in red chiripás, caps, and ponchos, they were strange fossils of a primitive past: "features as grave as arabs and old soldiers, their faces scarred and lined. A characteristic common to all, officers and men almost without exception, were their grey hairs, as though it had just snowed on their heads and beards. What mysteries of human nature, what terrible lessons for our people! . . . and for him, for Rosas, they had a profound affection, a veneration which they could hardly conceal."[15]

On their incorporation in the allied army, they were placed under the command of the unitarian Colonel Pedro León Aquino, Sarmiento's companion in exile and a close friend of Mitre. He acquired an untamable tiger. When the allies were crossing the pampas out of the territory of Santa Fe, on January 10, 1852, 400 of these men rebelled, killed their commander and other unitarian officers, and deserted to their true caudillo. Making their way through the pampas, they reached Santos Lugares and presented themselves triumphantly to Rosas, who warmly acknowledged their fealty.

Rosas, in short, was not isolated in Buenos Aires, and he could still count on the allegiance of the masses. Why, then, was there no popular rising in town and country on his behalf in 1852 that was comparable to the one in 1829? There were various reasons. In the first place, the essential support for Rosas in 1829 had come from the estancieros, who left nothing to chance but actively mobilized their peons for the caudillo's cause. Twenty years later many estancieros, their peons taken by conscription and their prospects worsened by war, preferred to remain aloof, waiting for peace and better times. Second, with his campaign of terror and total depoliticization of Buenos Aires, Rosas had taken the spontaneity out of such popular support as existed; if the prime mover failed, the machine stopped. Finally, there could be no mass rising in the countryside, as the regime's recruiting officers had already stripped it bare, and able-bodied men were either in the army or in hiding. So Rosas's last hope lay in the army.

The Battle of Buenos Aires

Rosas was not a great military commander, and he squandered his several assets. His defense measures were defeatist and delayed. He had lost two regular armies—Urquiza's and Oribe's—to the enemy. This loss was the result of a long-term strategic error whereby he had made the security of the regime dependent on the loyalty of provincial caudillos, concentrating his major defense effort on armies that he could not directly control and that in the event could easily be lost. A number of regional military chieftains also deserted him, and the forces of Santa Fe proved to be ineffective. He was forced back to his ultimate power base, the city and province of Buenos Aires. Yet even here it was not until November 1851 that he began to assemble a makeshift army, a combination of volunteers and conscripts raised in levies. However, there had been so many levies that his local officials found few men of military age left and could send him only teenage boys, dragged from their wailing mothers in scenes such as that described by W. H. Hudson, who observed a woman behaving "like some wild animal trying to save her offspring from the hunters."[16]

The militias of Buenos Aires and the countryside, now called the civil guard, were also makeshift forces, as people were forced to leave businesses, farms, and ranches to the detriment of production and trade. Artisans were employed on equipment, uniforms were ordered, and troops of horses were collected. Training was begun under retired officers recalled to the colors, and the face of the country was rapidly converted into a vast if disorderly encampment. The diarist Beruti recorded: "We ended the present year, 1851, with the misfortune of having all the inhabitants of the city and the province under arms, performing military exercises like soldiers, without distinction of clerks, lawyers, notaries, judges, and so on, capable of bearing arms, and even boys from twelve to sixteen years. . . . People have been brought in from the rural districts, rich and poor alike."[17] Rosas's best units were the artillery and the Regiment of Escort, though lacking good senior officers, he had to offer command of these units to two unitarian officers who had returned to Buenos Aires—Martiniano Chilavert, one of Lavalle's artillerymen in the campaign of 1840, and Pedro José Díaz, captured at Quebracho Herrado and on parole since then. They both accepted and in the last battle fought vigorously for Rosas. But the regime's greatest weakness was its lack of naval power. This lack enabled the Brazilians to dominate the Río de la Plata and all the other rivers and to provide effective transport and cover for the allied army. As late as January 17, 1852, Rosas bought, for £13,000, a British steamship of 395 tons to reinforce the squadron of Buenos Aires. By then it was too late.

If Rosas lacked military talents, some of his military chiefs lacked enthusiasm. He appointed Angel Pacheco commander of the vanguard and then commander in chief of the north and center of Buenos Aires. But Pacheco, hitherto a stalwart of the regime and one of its principal beneficiaries, seemed to have little stomach for the most crucial campaign of all. He was now alienated from Rosas and out of sympathy with his subordinate, Colonel Lagos, one of the commanders who still did his duty even raising 2,500 well-armed and mounted men from the districts of Luján, Chivilcoy, and 25 de Mayo. Pacheco had no plan and exercised no initiative. He did not engage the enemy; nor did he allow his subordinates to do so, and he failed to hold the bridge at Puente de Márquez. Instead he retreated further and then attempted to resign. His resignation was rejected, and on January 30, he left his station without consulting Rosas and withdrew to his estancia on the other side of the River Conchas. When the final battle of the regime was being fought, Pacheco and his cavalry force of 500 were resting on his estate. Thus, Urquiza had an open road to Buenos Aires all the way from Santa Fe. Meanwhile, in Buenos Aires itself, Rosas effectively lost the services of his commander, General Mansilla, who fell seriously ill on December 26 and became another of the regime's broken reeds.

Rosas was ignorant of the true situation, either through deception by his entourage or through its miscalculation. The British minister, Robert Gore, was present in the governor's house on the evening of February 2, and he was positively assured that General Nazario Benavídez, governor of San Juan, was in the rear of Urquiza's army with 4,000 men and that Pedro Rosas was in the rear of its right flank with 2,000 Indians; thus, Urquiza was caught between two fires. The information was totally false. And not only was Rosas deceived, he was virtually betrayed. A few days later, after the last battle, Gore reported: "Nearly all the chiefs in whom Rosas placed any confidence are now in the service employed by Urquiza, the same persons whom I have often heard swear devotion to the cause and person of General Rosas; no man was ever so betrayed. The confidential clerk that copied his notes and dispatches never failed in sending a copy to Urquiza of all that was interesting or important for him to know; the chiefs who commanded the vanguard of Rosas' army are now in command of districts. Never was treason more complete."[18]

Rosas had always ruled his own domain; now he had to fight his own battle, and it was a losing battle. He admitted that his army had insufficient officers, poor instructors, inexperienced troops. Arms and uniforms were being sent in all directions by any means available and invariably at the last minute. There was disorder in the ranks, confusion among commanders, and serious loss of morale. Rosas had to take command himself; there was hardly anyone else to do it, and no one he could trust.

During January 1852, Rosas was pinned down in Santos Lugares, unable to leave Buenos Aires in case the Brazilian reserve army stationed on the other side of the Río de la Plata at Colonia moved in and the city's defenders lacked the will to resist; eventually the Brazilians positioned 5,000 men outside the city. Rosas therefore did not move until Urquiza approached from the west. Then he decided to go out and meet him. On January 26, he delegated government to his ministers Arana and Manuel Insiarte. Military defense of the capital he left to Lucio Mansilla, now supposedly recovered, and to the urban militia. On January 27, he left Palermo and made his final dispositions at Santos Lugares; from there the army moved off in the hope of dealing a decisive blow to the enemy in a set battle. Thus on the night of February 2, Urquiza unexpectedly met the army of Rosas closing the road to Buenos Aires near the gully of Morón.

Caseros

On the night of February 2 with the enemy near and ready for battle, Rosas called a *junta de guerra*. He told his senior officers that honor and duty impelled him to direct the battle and that he would defend the rights and interests of the confederation to the last. But if they considered that he ought to negotiate for peace with Brazil and

Urquiza rather than fight, he would comply with their advice without thought for his own person. Martiniano Chilavert spoke for all when he said they should fight, and Rosas commended him for his patriotism, adding that whoever prevailed, Urquiza or Rosas, they should then work for a national constitution. "Our real enemy is the Empire of Brazil, because it is an Empire." But some officers, led by Chilavert, wanted further delaying tactics; they urged Rosas to pull back the infantry and artillery to cover the line of the city and to use the cavalry in mobile actions against the enemy rear guard. Others wanted an immediate battle in the morning. Rosas himself wanted action now, and he remarked to his aide, Antonino Reyes,

> I have been hearing the advice of the commanders on what we ought to do and each one has given me his opinion. They are of course against giving battle, and prefer to defend the city with the infantry and artillery and to send the cavalry to the south to raise the Indians. But you know that I am opposed to bringing in these elements, for if I am defeated I do not wish to leave the countryside in ruins. If we triumph, who will control the Indians? If we lose, who will control the Indians? . . . There is no other way; we have to play for high stakes and go for everything. Here we are, and from here there is no retreat.[19]

The two armies met on Tuesday, February 3, at Morón, a gully near the Río de las Conchas about twenty miles west of Buenos Aires. The army of Urquiza was 24,000 strong, of whom 3,500 were Brazilians, 1,500 Uruguayans, the rest Argentines; there were fifty pieces of artillery. The army of Rosas numbered 23,000 with fifty-six pieces of artillery. But there was no comparison between the veteran forces of Urquiza and the raw recruits of Rosas or between the respective high commands. Urquiza was a model of military experience and skill, whereas Rosas, for all his talent in irregular warfare, was not a professional soldier. His tactics were now as weak as his strategy; he had no obvious plans, and he positioned his troops indiscriminately. The battle began at 7 A.M. with artillery fire from both sides. Urquiza first attacked Rosas's left flank with his cavalry and scattered the enemy horses. He then deployed his infantry and artillery against Rosas's right flank, entrenched at the house of Caseros, from which the battle took its name; more resistance was offered there, but it too was overcome. So the forces of Rosas were easily outmaneuverd, surrounded, and dispersed; they fled in disarray, defeated as much by their lack of discipline, experience, and leadership as by the excellence of the allied army. Only Chilavert's artillery and Díaz's regiment put up an effective resistance, but they too were overcome. By midday, defeat was complete and readily conceded; total casualties were no more than 200, most of them in the army of Rosas. Thousands of troops with artillery, rifles, ammunition, stores, and equipment fell into the hands of the allies, and by 3 P.M. the victors were in Santos Lugares, which a few hours previously had been the military headquarters of a powerful regime.

Rosas's fall was swift and total. He suffered a slight hand wound and rode from the field of battle accompanied only by a servant to make his way to Hueco de los Sauces in the south of the city, where he wrote his resignation to the House of Representatives. Urquiza paid him a generous compliment: "Rosas is brave; during yesterday's battle I saw him at the front commanding his army."[20] But Sarmiento noticed how easy displacing Rosas had been in the end: "The defeat of the most feared tyrant of modern times has been accomplished in a single campaign, at the centre of his power, in one pitched battle, which opened the gates of the city, seat of his tyranny, and closed all possibility of prolonged resistance."

In Buenos Aires, as on the battlefield, the heat that day was overpowering. The distant sound of cannon had been heard from an early hour. At 9 A.M., rumors of a battle and the defeat of Rosas began to circulate, and at about 11 o'clock, groups of cavalry soldiers came galloping through, confirming the report. More fugitives arrived as the day went on, pausing only for refreshment before dispersing to the south. General Mansilla offered no defense, reluctant to use the civil guard to fight for the city; so the Brazilian reserve army did not even need to disembark. Instead, Mansilla withdrew the militia and asked the foreign diplomats to secure terms for Buenos Aires from Urquiza. Then, to the disgust of many, Rosas's brother-in-law surrendered to Urquiza with the cry, "Long live Urquiza! Death to the tyrant Rosas!" Soldiers from foreign vessels, including a party of British marines, landed to protect their nationals and property. But the only casualty was the master of HMS *Locust,* Mr. Payne, who against everyone's advice set off for Palermo to see what was happening. On the way, he was stopped by a fleeing soldier who demanded his horse and shot him when he refused; he later died on board ship. Meanwhile, the rout continued, and

Buenos Aires lay defenseless before the enemy. "Such was the inglo-
rious exit," concluded the London *Times* dispatch, "of the South
American tyrant; a dictator whose power was more absolute than
that of the Russian Autocrat, and of any earthly ruler."[21]

Soon Urquiza was in Palermo, where he established his headquarters. But in the city looting began, first by rosista cavalry, then
by Urquiza's troops and local delinquents, who formed roving
bands in the center of town, shooting doors open and plundering
shops. A breakdown of law and order threatened until Urquiza
imposed his authority and overcame terror by terror; in Buenos
Aires up to 200 were shot on his orders, including many civilians.
And victory was followed by a terrible vengeance. A number of senior rosista officers were shot, some for past terrorism, others with
less obvious justification. "The surviving *mazorqueros*," wrote
Sarmiento, "numbered six or seven, and the people of Buenos Aires
only held ill-will against the most criminal among them."[22] Colonel
Martín Isidro Santa Coloma, a hard-line rosista, had his throat cut
on Urquiza's orders; he had been a member of the mazorca, a justice of the peace, and a party to the assassination of Manuel Vicente
Maza in 1839. Martiniano Chilavert, a simple though senior officer who had changed sides, was also killed. Many troops were executed. The entire Aquino regiment, or those taken prisoner, were
killed without trial, and people applauded as they had their throats
cut. Around Palermo the trees were full of corpses. The infantry of
Rosas, recruited from the lower classes and with no voice in deci-
sionmaking, was held prisoner by Urquiza for about a month in
camps at Palermo. A number of rosista politicians, however, including Felipe Arana, Nicolás Anchorena, and Baldomero García, survived and prospered. Urquiza dispensed extremely rough justice,
sparing some, shooting others, cutting the throats of yet others, but
in general, like the terror of Rosas, retribution was a controlled
campaign.

Caseros did not signify the conquest of an old Argentina by a
new. Its immediate effect was to replace one caudillo with another.
Urquiza, whom a London *Times* correspondent in Buenos Aires
described as "more animal than intellectual" in expression, was in
some ways more of a gaucho than Rosas himself and only a degree
more conciliatory.[23] He set up his court at Palermo, ordered the
wearing of the federal uniform with red emblems in spite of its asso-

ciation with Rosas, and cried "Death to savage unitarians!"
Sarmiento saw him as another Rosas, surrounded by sycophants and
former rosistas. And in the aftermath of Caseros the victor seemed
destined to perpetuate the ideological conflicts and the caudillo politics of the time. According to the diarist Beruti, "A new tyrant,
replacing his master Rosas, has stationed his troops throughout the
city, giving the inhabitants a terrible fright. . . . Urquiza entered as
liberator and has become conqueror."[24]

Outside the city, folk memories and allegiances were stronger
and myths more tenacious. In the countryside and on the southern
frontier, throughout the former bases of his power, nostalgia for
Rosas became a form of protest. Gauchos saluted his memory, and
Indians invoked his name. In April 1852 about 200 Indians invaded
the province and threatened Bahía Blanca, raiding estancias for
horses and cattle. Robert Gore reported: "Small bodies of Indians
are daily joining the invaders, and last accounts give their numbers
as 2000, besides some Christians supposed to be part of the late
army of General Rosas. They have been reported to have cried at different times 'Viva Rosas' 'Muera Urquiza.' "[25] Rosas himself believed
that he had been defeated not by the people but by foreigners. He
asserted after Caseros, "It is not the people who have overthrown
me. It is the *macocos,* the Brazilians." And in a more cynical mood
he observed, "I am abandoned by everyone. The people hate me
because my generals and family have plundered them, and my generals abandon me because they are satiated with wealth and wish to
keep it."[26]

Could it be that the true explanation for the fall of Rosas has
a classical simplicity? He applied policies that were opposed outside Buenos Aires, if not within, and his opponents were strong
enough to defeat him. The Brazilians could not have invaded
Argentina without an ally within; and Urquiza could not have
rebelled without foreign support. Together they were too powerful
for Rosas. Suddenly he found himself alone. Economic life had to
go on. Ranchers had to produce and sell, sheep farmers had to
export, merchants had to trade, and they could carry on these
activities as well under another government as under Rosas. As for
the British, they had to find new partners and perhaps wider markets, and they too discovered that Rosas was not indispensable
after all.

Escape

After Caseros, Rosas's life was in danger. At the end of the battle, he said to his immediate companions, "Gentlemen, go your own way, I am leaving."[27] He insisted on going alone, accompanied by one servant, Lorenzo López; on his excellent horse Victoria—named after the Queen of England—he made his way quickly to the southern suburbs of the city. At the Hueco de los Sauces, he dismounted under a tree and wrote a formal resignation to the House of Representatives: "*Señores Representantes:* the time has come to return to you the office of governor of the Province and the sovereign powers with which you saw fit to honour me. I believe I have fulfilled my duty, as have all the true federalists and my companions in arms. If we have not done more in the sacred defence of our independence, of our integrity and of our honour, it is because we have not been able to do more."[28] Then, changing into the red poncho and scarlet hat of the soldier who accompanied him, Rosas entered the city and rode unrecognized to the home of Captain Robert Gore, RN, the British chargé d'affaires, in the calle Santa Rosa. He arrived about 4:00 P.M.

The escape had almost certainly been planned some days before. Gore approved of Rosas, if not of his methods, and he appreciated his provision of order and protection for foreigners. He seems to have had access to the dictator whenever he wished and in the last weeks of the regime was at Government House almost every day. He reported to Palmerston the possibility of Rosas's defeat, though not the existence of contingency plans. Later in exile, Rosas stated: "I had previously prepared everything for my departure, packing my papers and reaching agreement with the English minister."[29] His archives, in fact, had already been transferred to his town house, ready for transport. His daughter, Manuela, had also left Palermo the night before the battle. Defeat, if not presumed, was certainly anticipated.

Gore was out all day on February 3, conferring with other diplomats on the protection of their nationals and interests. When he returned home about 4:30 P.M. his servant informed him that he had admitted a person dressed as a common soldier, whom he suspected to be General Rosas. Gore found Rosas lying exhausted on his bed, hungry and with the dirt of battle still on him but otherwise calm and confident. He was happy to be under the protection of the British flag and was even disposed to stay a few days longer to put his affairs in order. Gore had some reservations about this intention, but he ordered his guest a meal and a bath; as he had to go out on further business with the victorious army, he left strict instructions that no one was to enter or leave the house until his return. Later that night, he called on Rear Admiral W. W. Henderson, commander of the British naval forces in the Río de la Plata, who readily agreed that it was vital to move Rosas from the chargé's residence, as his presence would be damaging to British interests, and that he should embark with his family at daybreak on board HMS *Locust,* which was then in port.

Gore now collected Manuela and took her to his house at midnight. There he convinced Rosas of the need to leave immediately, and preparations were put in hand. Gore provided Rosas with a sailor's greatcoat and hat; Manuelita dressed as a young boy; and Rosas's son put on some of their host's clothes. Thus disguised they went forth, escorted by Gore and six British marines. They were challenged twice at sentry posts but safely reached a boat on the river. By 3:00 A.M., they were all aboard the *Locust,* and from there they subsequently transferred to HMS *Centaur.* The next morning, Gore was presented to Urquiza, who remarked that Rosas had fought bravely and was now believed to be making his way south, a statement that Gore was not inclined to dispute.

Gore believed that he had only done his duty as an Englishman and a gentleman, acting on humanitarian principles. But in Buenos Aires there was some hostility toward him over Rosas's flight, and he was particularly incensed to observe that British residents were critical for his allegedly compromising them in the eyes of the victors. He reported to Palmerston that they threatened him in the street, demonstrated outside his house, and spread rumors that he had married Manuelita, received £12,000 in reward from Rosas, and taken over Palermo. But he treated all this gossip with the contempt it deserved and stood by his principles. He also denied stories of the wealth of Rosas, who had assured him that he had no money abroad and took with him only £2,300.

The provisional government in Buenos Aires, no less than the British authorities, was now anxious to speed the fallen dictator on his way. Rosas formally asked Admiral Henderson to be taken to

England, and on February 10 with his family, three servants, and a few colleagues he was transferred to the steamship HMS *Conflict* for the journey into exile. Rosas had a little money with him—745 ounces of gold, 200 gold pesos, 22 reales, as he declared. But he had his family to provide for, and it was assumed that he could not pay his passage or that of his party; in the event, the cost of the journey was borne by Britain. Rosas disembarked at Plymouth on April 26 and took up quarters at Moorshead's Royal Hotel, Devonport. The port authorities received him cordially; his arrival was greeted with a twenty-one-gun salute, he was met by various dignitaries, and his baggage was cleared quickly through customs. A reporter from the *Times* observed these events, and the newspaper voiced its disapproval of them: "Marvellous has been the eagerness of English gentlemen, high in military and naval authority, to grasp his blood-stained hand." Rosas wished to present himself to the British government and explain his position in person, and he also requested permission from the foreign secretary to rent a house in England. The foreign office did not encourage him to seek an interview; instead he received a letter acknowledging his right to settle in any part of the British Isles under the protection of existing laws and without need of special permission.

But questions were asked in the House of Lords. Why had General Rosas been given an apparently official reception at Plymouth? Why had he been received with more than the usual honors? The foreign secretary, the Earl of Malmesbury, replied that no order had been sent by the government directing official honors, but the authorities at Plymouth had acted on their own toward "no common refugee, but one who had shown great distinction and kindness to the British merchants who had traded with his country, and one with whom the late Government had carried on negotiations of an important character, and had even signed a Treaty in 1849." Discontent rumbled on, and the first lord of the admiralty had to explain that no special orders had been sent to the squadron in the River Plate, but there was a general order sent to all naval commanders to save life in emergencies such as that which had befallen General Rosas, and it was under these circumstances that he went on board the *Conflict*.[30]

Thus, Rosas passed from power in Argentina to private life in Britain, twenty years in office followed by twenty-five years in exile.

EPILOGUE

Rosas settled in England, first in Southampton then on a small farm at Swaythling, some three miles outside the town. Unlike many of his kind, he had not invested a fortune abroad, but he had enough to survive. On his farm, he could restore his identity, enjoy a few rural pursuits, make the rounds of his property, and indulge his liking for giving commands. As a perceptive observer remarked, "His greatest happiness seemed to be to sit on his horse and give orders to those employed."[1] He died on his farm on March 14, 1877, in his eighty-fourth year.

Exile did nothing to temper his rigid conservatism or to thaw the bleakness of his views. His political model remained that of enlightened despotism: "I have always admired autocratic dictators who have been the first servants of their people. That is my great title: I have always sought to serve the country."[2] He seems not to have had regrets about a single detail of his policy, and his conscience remained untroubled by even the most controversial actions of his government. The execution of Camila O'Gorman and her priest lover caused him not the slightest misgiving; it was justified for all time on the ground that moral anarchy needed absolute retribution. As he looked at the world around him in 1871, he uttered one of his most uncompromising statements of political belief: "When even the lower classes increasingly lose respect for law and order, and no longer fear divine punishment, only absolute powers are capable of imposing the laws of God and man, and respect for capital and its owners."[3]

Rosas followed the caudillo's classic route to power: he became a regional chieftain, sought and rewarded elite allies, seized the state, established a personal dictatorship, and survived through violence.

163

He came from the creole elite of land and militia, but his was not a passive inheritance; he enhanced these assets through his own initiative and, as a landowner and lord of many peons, created a power base that few could equal. He was not a soldier in the army of independence but acquired military experience in the conflicts of postwar Argentina, where the capacity to recruit forces for service on the frontier, in the pampas, or in the capital was more important than the ability to lead a regular army. He was a regional warlord before he was a servant of the state, and it could almost be said of Rosas that the state needed him more than he needed it.

Rosas was an elected governor and acquired legitimacy from the polls. The language of the regime was that of classical republicanism; the object was to restore the respect for order characteristic of the Spanish empire without the monarchical and colonial institutions on which it had been founded. Instead, the legitimacy and achievements of the Rosas regime were derived, in the eyes of its supporters, from its republican principles and virtues, embodied in its leader, Citizen Rosas.[4] But he dictated high terms for his appointment, exploiting people's horror of chaos and refusing to serve without absolute power. Of all the caudillos of Spanish America, Rosas was the most explicit in using the argument against anarchy. "When I took over the government I found the country in anarchy, divided into warring factions, reduced to pure chaos, a hell in miniature. . . . Before establishing a constitution, it was necessary to instil in the people habits of government and democratic ways, which was a long and arduous task."[5] This task took so long, in fact, that twenty years later he was still the sole power in the state. By virtue of the extraordinary powers vested in him, he bypassed the normal process of law and imposed a personal dictatorship in which he employed terror as a medium of government and cruelty as a form of persuasion. Through state terrorism, he destroyed the opposition and disciplined his own supporters. But he targeted his terrorism, sparing the popular classes and preserving his influence over them, an influence that people of property were happy to acknowledge. Outside the formal world of patron and client, many individuals, groups, and institutions in Argentina identified with Rosas. Estancieros saw a successful rancher, peons a gaucho chieftain, merchants an able businessman, townspeople a tireless administrator, priests an uncompromising traditionalist. Rosas had a comprehensive identity;

he reconciled the enmities in Argentine society and controlled its aggression. But he himself provoked hatred and opposition and in time prepared his own demise.

The economy flagged, and land use changed. Whereas the regime reflected a specific stage of development and served a particular social interest, Rosas was not a slave of the livestock economy, a captive of the estancia, or a man incapable of adjustment. Consequently, the shift from cattle estate to sheep farm was the framework rather than the cause of his downfall. Rosas was a casualty of political and military events that he helped to provoke and failed to anticipate. He applied policies that aroused opposition outside Buenos Aires, if not within, and his opponents were strong enough to defeat him. The Brazilians could not have invaded Argentina without an ally inside; and Urquiza could not have rebelled without foreign support. Together they were too powerful for Rosas. The caudillo who had neglected national organization and failed to rally the provinces to a greater Argentina at the end found himself isolated in a situation where personal sovereignty and individual allegiance were not enough and where his own client groups, conscious of a new balance of power, did not have the commitment or the will to save him. Personal dictatorship showed its strengths and its limits in Rosas.

Notes

Chapter 1, Pages 1–34

1. Adolfo Saldías, *Historia de la Confederación Argentina: Rosas y su época,* 9 vols. (Buenos Aires, 1958), 1:14–24.

2. Lucio V. Mansilla, *Rozas: Ensayo histórico-psicológico* (Paris, 1913), 21.

3. Emilio Ravignani, *Inferencias sobre Juan Manuel de Rosas y otros ensayos* (Buenos Aires, 1945), 51.

4. Henry Southern to Lord Palmerston, December 18, 1850, Historical Manuscripts Commission (HMC), London, Palmerston Papers, GC/SO/268.

5. Carlos Mayo, ed., *Pulperos y pulperías de Buenos Aires, 1740–1830* (Mar del Plata, Argentina, 1996), 25–42, 77–112, 139–50.

6. W. H. Hudson, *Far Away and Long Ago* (London, 1967), 54–55.

7. Leonardo León Solís, *Maloqueros y conchavadores en Araucanía y las Pampas, 1700–1800* (Temuco, Chile, 1990), 50–63, 200–206; Raúl Mandrini and Andrea Reguera, eds., *Huellas en la tierra: Indios, agricultores y hacendados en la pampa bonaerense* (Tandil, Argentina, 1993), 45–74.

8. Carlos Ibarguren, *Juan Manuel de Rosas: Su vida, su drama, su tiempo* (Buenos Aires, 1961), 44, 59, 87; Ernesto H. Celesia, *Rosas: Aportes para su historia,* 2d ed., 2 vols. (Buenos Aires, 1968), 1:54–55.

9. Charles Darwin, *Journal of Researches into the Natural History and Geology of the Countries Visited During the Voyage of H.M.S. "Beagle" Round the World,* 9th ed. (London, 1890), 85.

10. Alfredo J. Montoya, *Historia de los saladeros argentinos* (Buenos Aires, 1956), 50–54; Saldías, *Historia de la Confederación,* 1:221–34; Julio Irazusta, *Vida política de Juan Manuel de Rosas, a través de su correspondencia,* 8 vols. (Buenos Aires, 1970), 1:100–108.

11. "Manifiesto de Rosas," October 11, 1820, in Juan A. Pradere and Fermín Chávez, *Juan Manuel de Rosas,* 2 vols. (Buenos Aires, 1970), 1:26–28.

12. Enrique M. Barba, *Como llegó Rosas al poder* (Buenos Aires, 1972), 8.

13. *El Lucero,* no. 78, December 9, 1829, enclosed in Woodbine Parish to Lord Aberdeen, December 12, 1829, Public Record Office (PRO), London, Foreign Office (FO) 6/27.

14. On the "career of the revolution" see Tulio Halperín Donghi, *Politics, Economics and Society in Argentina in the Revolutionary Period* (Cambridge, England, 1975), 211–15, 382–91.

15. Mansilla, *Rozas,* 145.

16. Saldías, *Historia de la Confederación,* 1:25–26.

Chapter 2, Pages 35–58

1. Domingo Faustino Sarmiento, *Inmigración y colonización,* in *Obras de D. F. Sarmiento,* 53 vols. (Santiago and Buenos Aires, 1866–1914), 23:292.

2. Arturo Enrique Sampay, *Las ideas políticas de Juan Manuel de Rosas* (Buenos Aires, 1972), 129–36.

3. Charles Darwin, *Journal of Researches into the Natural History and Geology of the Countries Visited During the Voyage of H.M.S. "Beagle" Round the World,* 9th ed. (London, 1890), 96.

4. Juan Manuel de Rosas, *Diario de la expedición al desierto (1833–1834)* (Buenos Aires, 1965), 55.

5. Order of the day, March 11, 1833, in Julio Irazusta, *Vida política de Juan Manuel de Rosas, a través de su correspondencia,* 8 vols. (Buenos Aires, 1970), 2:203.

6. Darwin, *Journal,* 51.

7. Rosas, *Diario,* 136–37.

8. Hamilton to Wellington, February 14, 1835, PRO, FO 6/46.

9. *Gaceta Mercantil,* July 1835, in Antonio Zinny, *La Gaceta Mercantil de Buenos Aires, 1823–1852,* 3 vols. (Buenos Aires, 1912), 2:244–45.

10. William MacCann, *Two Thousand Miles' Ride Through the Argentine Provinces,* 2 vols. (London, 1853), 1:86.

11. Miron Burgin, *The Economic Aspects of Argentine Federalism 1820–1852* (Cambridge, MA, 1946), 255.

12. Ernesto Quesada, *La época de Rosas: Su verdadero carácter histórico* (Buenos Aires, 1923), 78–79.

13. Irazusta, *Vida política de Juan Manuel de Rosas,* 1:161; Ernesto Quesada, *Acha y la batalla de Angaco* (Buenos Aires, 1965), 22–23.

14. Wilfrid Latham, *The States of the River Plate,* 2d ed. (London, 1868), 316.

15. Juan José Sebreli, *Apogeo y ocaso de los Anchorena* (Buenos Aires, 1972), 167.

16. Jonathan C. Brown, *A Socioeconomic History of Argentina, 1776–1860* (Cambridge, England, 1979), 154.

17. Antonio Dellepiane, *El testamento de Rosas* (Buenos Aires, 1957), 101–102. On the Anchorena cattle business see Brown, *A Socioeconomic History of Argentina,* 171–200; it gives their total holdings by 1864 as 9,582 square kilometers.

18. Andrés M. Carretero, *La propiedad de la tierra en la época de Rosas* (Buenos Aires, 1972), 60–160.

19. MacCann, *Two Thousand Miles' Ride*, 2:8.
20. Dellepiane, *El testamento de Rosas*, 96.
21. Darwin, *Journal*, 52–53, 85.
22. Archivo Histórico de la Provincia de Buenos Aires, *Mensajes de los gobernadores de la provincia de Buenos Aires 1822–1849*, 2 vols. (La Plata, Argentina, 1976), 2:271.
23. Hilda Sabato, *Agrarian Capitalism and the World Market: Buenos Aires in the Pastoral Age, 1840–1890* (Albuquerque, 1990), 23–39.
24. The outstanding modern work on estancias is Samuel Amaral, *The Rise of Capitalism on the Pampas: The Estancias of Buenos Aires, 1785–1870* (Cambridge, England, 1998), which shows that their expansion was due not only to well-known external factors such as the growing demand for hides but also to high-level management skills.
25. Domingo Faustino Sarmiento, *Campaña en el ejército grande aliado de Sud América*, ed. Tulio Halperín Donghi (Mexico City, Buenos Aires, 1958), 241.

Chapter 3, Pages 35–57

1. William MacCann, *Two Thousand Miles' Ride Through the Argentine Provinces*, 2 vols. (London, 1853), 1:158. Jonathan Brown draws attention to the diversity of the rural population and estimates at 35 percent those who did not work directly on the land (in 1854); see *A Socioeconomic History of Argentina 1776–1860* (London, 1853), 155–56.
2. Adolfo Saldías, ed., *Papeles de Rozas*, 2 vols. (La Plata, Argentina, 1904–1907), 2:253–54.
3. Lucio V. Mansilla, *Rozas: Ensayo histórico-psicológico* (Paris, 1913), 145.
4. Rosas to Felipe Arana, August 28, 1833, in Ernesto H. Celesia, *Rosas: Aportes para su historia*, 2d ed., 2 vols. (Buenos Aires, 1968), 1:530.
5. Rosas to Josefa Gómez, September 24, 1871, in Carlos Ibarguren, *Juan Manuel de Rosas: Su vida, su drama, su tiempo* (Buenos Aires, 1961), 306.
6. Domingo Faustino Sarmiento, *Facundo* (La Plata, Argentina, 1938), 44–45, 53–63, 65.
7. Wilfrid Latham, *The States of the River Plate*, 2d ed. (London, 1868), 326–27.
8. Rosas to provincial government, in Alfredo J. Montoya, *Historia de los saladeros argentinos* (Buenos Aires, 1956), 41.
9. Arturo Enrique Sampay, *Las ideas políticas de Juan Manuel de Rosas* (Buenos Aires, 1972), 131–32.
10. Gregorio F. Rodríguez, ed. *Contribución histórica y documental*, 3 vols. (Buenos Aires, 1921–1922), 2:467–68.
11. Charles Darwin, *Journal of Researches . . . During the Voyage of H.M.S. "Beagle" Round the World*, 9th ed. (London, 1890), 53, 113–14.

12. Andrés Lamas, "Agresiones de Rosas," in Angel J. Carranza, ed., *Escritos políticos y literarios durante la guerra contra la tiranía de D. Juan Manuel de Rosas* (Buenos Aires, 1877), 27, 367.

13. Philip Yorke Gore to Lord Palmerston, October 21, 1833, PRO, FO 6/37; John Henry Mandeville to Lord Aberdeen, July 7, 1842, PRO, FO 6/84; Henry Southern to Lord Palmerston, November 22, 1848, HMC, London, Palmerston Papers, GC/SO/241.

14. Sarmiento, *Facundo,* 68.

15. Gregorio Araoz de La Madrid, *Memorias,* 2 vols. (Buenos Aires, 1968), 1:199.

16. For another interpretation, which places collective action from below ahead of the action of Rosas in 1829, see Pilar González Bernaldo, "El levantamiento de 1829: El imaginario social y sus implicaciones políticas en un conflicto rural," in *Anuario del IEHS* (Instituto de Estudios Histórico Sociales) no. 2 (Tandil, 1987), 137–76.

17. General J. T. O'Brien to Aberdeen, January 1845, PRO, FO 6/110.

18. Rosas to Doña Encarnación, November 23, 1833, in *Revista Argentina de Ciencias Políticas* 28 (1958):118–26.

19. William Gore Ouseley to Lord Aberdeen, July 26, 1845, PRO, FO 6/104.

20. MacCann, *Two Thousand Miles' Ride,* 1:154. MacCann uses the terms "native peon or labourer," "native peasant."

21. Rosas, *Mensaje,* January 1, 1837, in Archivo Histórico de la Provincia de Buenos Aires, *Mensajes de los gobernadores de la provincia de Buenos Aires, 1822–1849,* 2 vols. (La Plata, Argentina, 1976), 1:109.

22. Benito Díaz, *Juzgados de paz de campaña de la provincia de Buenos Aires (1821–1854)* (La Plata, Argentina, 1959), 133.

23. John Henry Mandeville to Strangways, October 18, 1836, PRO, FO 6/53.

24. MacCann, *Two Thousand Miles' Ride,* 1:162–63.

25. Xavier Marmier, *Buenos Aires y Montevideo en 1852,* trans. and ed. José Luis Busaniche (Buenos Aires, 1948), 75.

26. Gore to Palmerston, December 12, 1833, in *British and Foreign State Papers* (London, 1832), 23:131–132.

27. Andrew Thorndike to Rosas, December 11, 1840, Archivo General de la Nación (AGN) Buenos Aires, Sala 10, 17-3-2, Gobierno, Solicitudes, Embargos.

28. Manigot and Meslin to Rosas, February 24, 1841, AGN, Sala 10, 17-3-2, Gobierno, Solicitudes, Embargos.

29. Henry Southern to Lord Palmerston, July 28, 1851, PRO, FO 6/158.

30. *El Grito Argentino,* Montevideo, February 24, 1839.

31. La Madrid, *Memorias,* 1:198–99.

32. Southern to Palmerston, October 18, 1848, PRO, FO 6/139.

33. Rosas, *Mensaje,* December 31, 1835, in *Mensajes de los gobernadores,* 1:83–84.

Chapter 4, Pages 59–73

1. Juan Carlos Nicolau, *Industria argentina y aduana 1835–1854* (Buenos Aires, 1975), 52–56.
2. Woodbine Parish, *Buenos Ayres and the Provinces of the Río de la Plata*, 2d ed. (London, 1852), 362.
3. "Projecto de Juan Manuel de Rosas sobre la escasez y la carestía de la carne," May 5, 1818, in Arturo Enrique Sampay, *Las ideas políticas de Juan Manuel de Rosas* (Buenos Aires, 1972), 89–96.
4. Pedro Ferré, *Memoria del brigadier general Pedro Ferré, octubre de 1821 a diciembre de 1842* (Buenos Aires, 1921), 52.
5. Text in ibid., 366–71.
6. Circular letter of Ferré to governments of the interior, April 13, 1832, *Documentos para la historia argentina* (Buenos Aires, 1913), 17:154–65.
7. Ferré, *Memoria*, 55.
8. Tulio Halperín Donghi, *Politics, Economics and Society in Argentina in the Revolutionary Period* (Cambridge, England, 1975), 89–91.
9. José M. Mariluz Urquijo, *Estado e industria 1810–1862* (Buenos Aires, 1969), 65–66.
10. Pedro de Angelis, "Memoria sobre el estado de la hacienda pública," in Urquijo, *Estado e industria 1810–1862*, 101–108.
11. H. S. Ferns, *Britain and Argentina in the Nineteenth Century* (Oxford, 1960), 251–52.
12. Miron Burgin, *The Economic Aspects of Argentine Federalism 1820–1852* (Cambridge, MA, 1946), 237, 240, 242, 263–64.
13. *Mensaje,* December 31, 1835, in Archivo Histórico de la Provincia de Buenos Aires, *Mensajes de los gobernadores de la provincia de Buenos Aires 1822–1849,* 2 vols. (La Plata, Argentina, 1976), 1:95.
14. Rosas to Rafael Atienza, July 20, 1836, in Academia Nacional de la Historia, *Historia de la Nación Argentina,* ed. Ricardo Levene, 2d ed. (Buenos Aires, 1951), vol. 7, part 2, 147.
15. Rosas, *Mensaje,* January 1, 1837, *Mensajes de los gobernadores,* 1:113.

Chapter 5, Pages 75–93

1. Rosas to Estanislao López, January 23, 1836, in Enrique M. Barba, ed., *Correspondencia entre Rosas, Quiroga y López* (Buenos Aires, 1958), 310.
2. Rosas, interview with Vicente G. and Ernesto Quesada, Southampton, 1873, in Arturo Enrique Sampay, *Las ideas políticas de Juan Manuel de Rosas* (Buenos Aires, 1972), 215, 218–19.
3. Rosas to López, May 17, 1832, October 1, 1835, in Barba, *Correspondencia entre Rosas, Quiroga y López,* 158, 267.

4. Rosas to Facundo Quiroga, February 28, 1832, in Enrique M. Barba, "El primer gobierno de Rosas," Academia Nacional de la Historia, *Historia de la Nación Argentina,* 7, 2:5.

5. Enrique Lafuente to Félix Frías, April 18, 1839, in Gregorio F. Rodríguez, ed., *Contribución histórica y documental,* 3 vols. (Buenos Aires, 1921–1922), 2: 468–69.

6. Mark D. Szuchman, *Order, Family, and Community in Buenos Aires 1810–1860* (Stanford, 1988), 219–23.

7. Ernesto H. Celesia, *Rosas: Aportes para su historia,* 2d ed., 2 vols. (Buenos Aires, 1968), 2:172–77.

8. Ibid.

9. Antonio Zinny, *La Gaceta Mercantil de Buenos Aires, 1823–1852,* 3 vols. (Buenos Aires, 1912), 2:236.

10. Rosas to López, January 23, 1836, in Enrique M.Barba, "Formación de la tiranía," Academia Nacional de la Historia, *Historia de la Nación Argentina,* 7, 2:134; Henry Southern to Lord Palmerston, Private, January 27, 1850, HMC, London, Palmerston Papers, GC/SO/251.

11. Rosas, circular letter to provincial governors, April 20, 1835, in Archivo Histórico de Santa Fe, *Papeles de Rosas 1821–1850* (Santa Fe, Argentina, 1928), 58–59.

12. Rosas to Quiroga, Hacienda de Figueroa, December 20, 1834, in Andrés M. Carretero, ed., *El pensamiento político de Juan M. de Rosas* (Buenos Aires, 1970), 70–78.

13. Casto Cáceres to Rosas, October 9, 1840, in Martiniano Leguizamón, *Papeles de Rosas* (Buenos Aires, 1935), 32–34.

14. Raúl Héctor Castagnino, *Rosas y los Jesuítas* (Buenos Aires, 1970), 50.

15. Southern to Palmerston, July 16, 1849, PRO, FO 6/144.

16. Southern to Palmerston, October 18, 1848, PRO, FO 6/139.

17. Lafuente to Frías, April 1839, in Rodríguez, *Contribución histórica y documental,* 2:461.

18. William MacCann, *Two Thousand Miles' Ride Through the Argentine Provinces,* 2 vols. (London, 1853), 2:20–21.

19. John Henry Mandeville to Lord Palmerston, May 2, 1838, PRO, FO 6/64.

20. Xavier Marmier, *Buenos Aires y Montevideo en 1852,* trans. and ed. José Luis Busaniche (Buenos Aires, 1948), 21.

21. Southern to Palmerston, November 21, 1848, PRO, FO 6/139.

22. Thomas Hobbes, *Leviathan* (London, 1976), 89–90.

Chapter 6, Pages 95–119

1. José Antonio Linera to Rosas, October 31, 1839, AGN, Colección Celesia, 22-1-12, f. 315.

2. Cuartel General en Dolores, November 5, 1839, AGN, Archivo Adolfo Saldías, Sala 7, 3-3-81, f. 126–29.

3. Enrique Lafuente to Félix Frías, April 1839, in Gregorio F. Rodríguez, ed., *Contribucion histórica y documental,* 3 vols. (Buenos Aires, 1921–1922), 2:458.

4. John Henry Mandeville to Strangways, October 18, 1836, PRO, FO 6/53.

5. Domingo Faustino Sarmiento, *Facundo* (La Plata, Argentina, 1938), 76.

6. W. H. Hudson, *Far Away and Long Ago* (London, 1967), 107.

7. Sarmiento, *Facundo,* 77.

8. Juan Manuel Beruti, *Memorias curiosas,* vol. 4 of *Biblioteca de Mayo* (Buenos Aires, 1960), 4134.

9. General J. T. O'Brien to Lord Aberdeen, January 1845, PRO, FO 6/110.

10. Julián González Salomón to Rosas, September 30, 1840, Rosas to Salomón, September 30, 1840, AGN, Colección Celesia, 22-1-13, f. 160–62; Ernesto Celesia, *Rosas: Aportes para su historia,* 2d ed., 2 vols. (Buenos Aires, 1968), 2: 235–37.

11. Esteban Echeverría, *Obras completas,* 5 vols. (Buenos Aires, 1870–1874), 4:40.

12. Adolfo Saldías, *Historia de la Confederación Argentina: Rosas y su época,* 9 vols. (Buenos Aires, 1958), 5: 48.

13. Henry Southern to Lord Palmerston, July 16, 1849, PRO, FO 6/144.

14. Emilio Ravignani, *Rosas: Interpretación real y moderna* (Buenos Aires, 1970), 75–76; *Inferencias sobre Juan Manuel de Rosas y otros ensayos* (Buenos Aires, 1945), 25–35.

15. Martiniano Leguizamón, *Papeles de Rosas* (Buenos Aires, 1935), 126.

16. Manuel Corvalán to Vicente González, September 10, 1840, in Antonio Zinny, *La Gaceta Mercantil de Buenos Aires, 1823–1852,* 3 vols. (Buenos Aires, 1912), 2:436.

17. Antonio Díaz, *Historia política y militar de las repúblicas del Plata,* 12 vols. (Montevideo, 1877–1878), 5: 96.

18. John Henry Mandeville to Palmerston, September 23, 1840, PRO, FO 6/75.

19. Mandeville to Rosas, October 9, 1840. Adolfo Saldías, *Papeles de Rozas,* 2 vols. (La Plata, Argentina, 1904–1907), 1:207, 462; *Historia de la Confederación,* 5:229.

20. Rosas to Mandeville, October 10, 1840, AGN, Archivo Adolfo Saldías, Sala 7, 3-3-8, f. 316–18; Saldías, *Historia de la Confederación,* 5: 230–34.

21. Mandeville to Palmerston, October 14, 1840, PRO, FO 6/75.

22. Rosas to López, governor of Córdoba, January 20, 1841, in Ernesto Quesada, *La época de Rosas: Su verdadero carácter histórico* (Buenos Aires, 1923), 107.

23. Quesada, *La época de Rosas,* 105–106.

24. Díaz, *Historia política y militar de las repúblicas del Plata,* 5: 96–97.

25. Mandeville to Charles John Canning, April 18, 1842, PRO, FO 6/83.

26. Mandeville to Canning, April 24, 1842, PRO, FO 6/83.

27. Mandeville to Aberdeen, July 7, 1842, PRO, FO 6/84.

28. Beruti, *Memorias curiosas,* 4066.

29. Southern to Palmerston, October 18, 1848, PRO, FO 6/139.

30. John Masefield, *Rosas.*

31. Rosas to Federico Terrero, Southampton, March 6, 1870, in Saldías, *Historia de la Confederación,* 8: 227–28; Lucio V. Mansilla, *Rozas: Ensayo histórico-psicológico* (Paris, 1913), 171–72.

32. Southern to Palmerston, November 24, 1848, PRO, FO 6/139.

33. Beruti, *Memorias curiosas,* 4077.

34. Southern to Palmerston, June 25, 1851, PRO, FO 6/158.

35. Mansilla, *Rozas: Ensayo histórico-psicológico,* 85.

36. *Causa criminal seguida contra el ex-gobernador Juan Manuel de Rosas entre los tribunales ordinarios de Buenos Aires* (Buenos Aires, 1908), 13–14.

Chapter 7, Pages 121–138

1. *Archivo Americano,* new series, no. 3, 501–31.

2. Andrés Bello to Baldomero García, December 30, 1846, in Julio Irazusta, *Vida política de Juan Manuel de Rosas: A través de su correspondencia,* 8 vols. (Buenos Aires, 1970), 5:205.

3. Juan Manuel Beruti, *Memorias curiosas,* vol. 4 of *Biblioteca de Mayo* (Buenos Aires, 1960), 4059, 4066.

4. Henry Southern to Lord Palmerston, November 21, 1848, PRO, FO 6/139.

5. Adolfo Saldías, *Historia de la Confederación Argentina: Rosas y su época,* 9 vols. (Buenos Aires, 1958), 8:94.

6. Southern to Palmerston, July 16, 1849, PRO, FO 6/144.

7. Southern to Palmerston, October 18, 1848, PRO, FO 6/139.

8. William MacCann, *Two Thousand Miles' Ride Through the Argentine Provinces,* 2 vols. (London, 1853), 2:5,9.

9. Southern to Palmerston, November 26, 1849, HMC, London, Palmerston Papers, GC/SO/248.

10. Southern to Palmerston, November 22, 1848, HMC, GC/SO/241.

11. Southern to Palmerston, March 6, 1849, HMC, GC/SO/243.

12. Ernesto Celesia, *Rosas: Aportes para su historia,* 2d ed., 2 vols. (Buenos Aires, 1968), 2:512.

13. Southern to Palmerston, June 25, 1851, PRO, FO 6/158.

14. Rosas, *Mensaje,* December 27, 1849, in Archivo Histórico de la Provincia de Buenos Aires, *Mensajes de los gobernadores de la provincia de Buenos Aires, 1822–1849,* 2 vols. (La Plata, Argentina, 1976), 2:269–70.

15. Southern to Palmerston, October 11, 1849, PRO, FO 6/145; Robert Gore to Palmerston, February 2, 1852, PRO, FO 6/167.

16. Celesia, *Rosas: Aportes para su historia,* 2:194–98.

17. Saldías, *Historia de la Confederación,* 8:180.

18. *Registro Oficial,* libro 29, 1850, 15.

19. *Comercio del Plata,* no. 1614, June 8, 1851.

20. Jorge M. Mayer, *Alberdi y su tiempo* (Buenos Aires, 1963), 381.

21. Quoted in José María Rosa, *La caída de Rosas,* 2d ed. (Buenos Aires, 1968), 67.

22. Celesia, *Rosas: Aportes para su historia,* 2:281–285.

23. Southern to Palmerston, July 18, 1850, HMC, London, Palmerston Papers, GC/SO/267.

24. Southern to Palmerston, January 10, 1851, PRO, FO 6/157.

25. Celesia, *Rosas: Aportes para su historia,* 2:293–323.

26. Ibid.

27. Rosas, Interview with Vicente Quesada, February 1873, in Ernesto Quesada, *La época de Rosas: Su verdadero carácter histórico* (Buenos Aires, 1923), 230–31.

28. Sarmiento, *El Progreso,* October 8, 1844, in *Obras de D. F. Sarmiento,* 53 vols. (Santiago and Buenos Aires, 1866–1914), 6:118–19; *Juan Manuel de Rosas: Su política, su caída, su herencia,* vol. 3 of *Obras selectas,* ed. Enrique de Gandia (Buenos Aires, 1944), 103–106.

29. Sarmiento, *Facundo,* 303.

30. Juan Bautista Alberdi, *La República Argentina: Treinta y siete años después de su Revolución,* Valparaiso, May 25, 1847, *Obras completas,* 8 vols. (Buenos Aires, 1886–1887), 3:223, 225, 241.

31. Southern to Palmerston, January 18, 1851, PRO, FO 6/157.

32. Florencio Varela, *Rosas y su gobierno* (Buenos Aires, 1929), 65.

Chapter 8, Pages 139–162

1. Henry Southern to Lord Palmerston, October 19, 1850, PRO, FO 6/152.

2. José María Rosa, *La caída de Rosas,* 2d ed. (Buenos Aires, 1968), 246–47, 335–45.

3. Beatriz Bosch, *Urquiza y su tiempo* (Buenos Aires, 1971), 171–72.

4. Ernesto H. Celesia, *Rosas: Aportes para su historia,* 2d ed., 2 vols. (Buenos Aires, 1968), 2:347.

5. Bosch, *Urquiza y su tiempo,* 191–92, 205–6.

6. Southern to Palmerston, November 2, 1851, PRO, FO 6/160.

7. Rosa, *La caída de Rosas,* 593–94.

8. Florencia Varela, *Rosas y su gobierno (escritos políticos, económicos y literarios)* (Buenos Aires, 1927), 102–3.

9. Proclamation of Urquiza, December 10, 1851, in Celesia, *Rosas: Aportes para su historia,* 2:506–7.

10. Domingo Faustino Sarmiento, *Campaña en el ejército grande aliado de Sud América,* ed. Tulio Halperín Donghi (Mexico City, Buenos Aires, 1958), 141, 144, 186–87.

11. Southern to Palmerston, November 22, 1848, HMC, London, Palmerston Papers, GC/SO/241.

12. Robert Gore to Palmerston, January 4, February 2, 1852, PRO, FO 6/167.

13. César Díaz, *Memorias, 1842–1852: Arroyo Grande; sitio de Montevideo; Caseros* (Buenos Aires, 1943), 220–223, 229, 237, 269.

14. Quoted in Carlos Ibarguren, *Juan Manuel de Rosas: Su vida, su drama, su tiempo* (Buenos Aires, 1961), 284.

15. Sarmiento, *Campaña en el ejército grande,* 100–101.

16. W. H. Hudson, *Far Away and Long Ago* (London, 1967), 99–100.

17. Juan Manuel Beruti, *Memorias curiosas,* vol. 4 of *Biblioteca de Mayo* (Buenos Aires, 1960), 4088.

18. Gore to Palmerston, February 9, 1852, HMC, London, Palmerston Papers, GC/GO/64; see also Gore to Palmerston, February 9, 1852, PRO, FO 6/167, and HMC, Palmerston Papers, GC/GO/65.

19. Report of Antonino Reyes, in Academia Nacional de la Historia, *Partes de Batalla de las guerras civiles 1840–1852,* 3 vols. (Buenos Aires, 1977), 3:412.

20. Julio Irazusta, *Vida política de Juan Manuel de Rosas: A través de su correspondencia,* 8 vols. (Buenos Aires, 1970), 8:314.

21. "From a private letter" dated Buenos Aires, February 3, 1852, *Times* (London), April 27, 1852.

22. Sarmiento, *Campaña en el ejército grande,* 211–12.

23. "From a Private Letter," *Times* (London), April 27, 1852.

24. Beruti, *Memorias curiosas,* 4107.

25. Gore to Earl of Malmesbury, April 29, 1852, PRO, FO/167.

26. Quoted in Ernesto J. Fitte, "Después de Caseros," *Historia* 30 (1963):103.

27. Reyes, *Partes de Batalla,* 3:416.

28. Adolfo Saldías, ed., *Papeles de Rozas,* 2 vols. (La Plata, Argentina, 1904–1907), 2:246–48.

29. Interview with Vicente V. Quesada, February 1873, in Ernesto Quesada, *La época de Rosas: Su verdadero carácter histórico* (Buenos Aires, 1923), 231.

30. House of Lords, April 29, 1852, *Parliamentary Debates,* 3d Series, 120:1279–82.

Epilogue, Pages 163–165

1. Obituary of Rosas, *Times* (London), March 15, 1877.

2. Interviews with Vicente Quesada, February 1873, in Ernesto Quesada, *La época de Rosas: Su verdadero carácter histórico* (Buenos Aires, 1923), 231–32.

3. Rosas to Josefa Gómez, September 24, 1871; José Raed, ed., *Cartas del exilio, 1853–1875* (Buenos Aires, 1974), 166–67.

4. Jorge Myers, *Orden y virtud: El discurso republicano en el régimen rosista* (Buenos Aires, 1995), 74–75, 305–8.

5. Rosas, interview with Quesada, February 1873, in Quesada, *La época de Rosas,* 230–31.

BIBLIOGRAPHY

Rosas: Life and Times

Bethell, Leslie, ed. *Argentina Since Independence.* Cambridge, England, 1993.

Ibarguren, Carlos. *Juan Manuel de Rosas: Su vida, su drama, su tiempo.* Buenos Aires, 1961.

Irazusta, Julio. *Vida política de Juan Manuel de Rosas, a través de su correspondencia.* 8 vols. Buenos Aires, 1970.

Mansilla, Lucio V. *Rozas: Ensayo histórico-psicológico.* Paris, 1913.

Ravignani, Emilio. *Rosas: Interpretación real y moderna.* Buenos Aires, 1970.

Shumway, Nicolas. *The Invention of Argentina.* Berkeley, 1991.

Politics

Barba, Enrique M. *Como llegó Rosas al poder.* Buenos Aires, 1972.

Bushnell, David. *Reform and Reaction in the Platine Provinces, 1810–1852.* Gainesville, 1983.

Celesia, Ernesto H. *Rosas: Aportes para su historia.* 2d ed., 2 vols. Buenos Aires, 1968.

Halperín Donghi, Tulio. *Argentina: De la revolución de independencia a la confederación rosista.* Buenos Aires, 1972.

——. *Politics, Economics and Society in Argentina in the Revolutionary Period.* Cambridge, England, 1975.

Quesada, Ernesto. *La época de Rosas: Su verdadero carácter histórico.* Buenos Aires, 1923.

Rosa, José María. *La caída de Rosas.* 2d ed. Buenos Aires, 1968.

Saldías, Adolfo. *Historia de la Confederación Argentina: Rosas y su época.* 9 vols. Buenos Aires, 1958.

Sampay, Arturo Enrique. *Las ideas políticas de Juan Manuel de Rosas.* Buenos Aires, 1972.

Economy

Brown, Jonathan C. *A Socioeconomic History of Argentina, 1776–1860.* Cambridge, England, 1979.

Burgin, Miron. *The Economic Aspects of Argentine Federalism 1820–1852.* Cambridge, MA, 1946.

Ferns, H. S. *Britain and Argentina in the Nineteenth Century.* Oxford, 1960.

Halperín Donghi, Tulio. *Guerra y finanzas en los orígenes del estado argentino (1791–1850).* Buenos Aires, 1982.

Nicolau, Juan Carlos. *Industria argentina y aduana 1835–1854.* Buenos Aires, 1975.

Reber, Vera Blinn. *British Mercantile Houses in Buenos Aires, 1810–1880.* Cambridge, MA, 1979.

Society

Andrews, George Reid. *The Afro-Argentines of Buenos Aires, 1800–1900.* Madison, WI, 1980.

Carretero, Andrés M. *La propiedad de la tierra en la época de Rosas.* Buenos Aires, 1972.

Gori, Gastón. *Vagos y mal entretenidos.* 2d ed. Santa Fe, 1965.

Molas, Ricardo. *Historia social del gaucho.* Buenos Aires, 1968.

Slatta, Richard. *Gauchos and the Vanishing Frontier.* Lincoln, NE, 1983.

Zorrilla, Rubén H. *Extracción social de los caudillos 1810–1870.* Buenos Aires, 1972.

Historical and Literary Sources

Beruti, Juan Manuel. *Memorias curiosas.* Vol. 4 of *Biblioteca de Mayo.* Buenos Aires, 1960.

Cunninghame Graham, R. B. *Thirteen Stories.* London, 1900.

Hudson, W. H. *Far Away and Long Ago.* London, 1967.

MacCann, William. *Two Thousand Miles' Ride Through the Argentine Provinces.* 2 vols. London, 1853.

Parish, Woodbine, *Buenos Ayres and the Provinces of the Rio de la Plata.* 2d ed. London, 1852.

Sarmiento, Domingo Faustino. *Facundo.* La Plata, 1938. There is an English translation by Mrs. Horace Mann, *Life in the Argentine Republic in the Days of the Tyrants: or Civilization and Barbarism,* New York, 1868.

Recent Research

Amaral, Samuel. *The Rise of Capitalism on the Pampas: The Estancias of Buenos Aires, 1785–1870.* Cambridge, England, 1998.

Chiaramonte, José Carlos. *Ciudades, provincias, estados: Orígenes de la nacion argentina (1800–1846).* Buenos Aires, 1997.

González Bernaldo de Quirós, Pilar. *Civilité et politique aux origines de la nation argentine: Les sociabilités à Buenos Aires 1829–1862.* Paris, 1999.

Lynch, John. *Caudillos in Spanish America 1800–1850.* Oxford, 1992.

Mayo, Carlos A. *Estancia y sociedad en la pampa,1740–1820.* Buenos Aires, 1995.

Myers, Jorge. *Orden y virtud: El discurso republicano en el régimen rosista.* Buenos Aires, 1995.

Sabato, Hilda. *Agrarian Capitalism and the World Market: Buenos Aires in the Pastoral Age, 1840–1890.* Albuquerque, 1990.

Szuchman, Mark D. *Order, Family, and Community in Buenos Aires 1810–1860.* Stanford, 1988.

Szuchman, Mark D., and Jonathan C. Brown, eds. *Revolution and Restoration: The Rearrangement of Power in Argentina, 1776–1860.* Lincoln, NE, 1994.

INDEX

Latin American Silhouettes
Studies in History and Culture

William H. Beezley and
Judith Ewell
Editors

Volumes Published

Silvia Marina Arrom and Servando Ortoll, eds., *Riots in the Cities: Popular Politics and the Urban Poor in Latin America, 1765–1910* (1996). Cloth ISBN 0-8420-2580-4   Paper ISBN 0-8420-2581-2

Roderic Ai Camp, ed., *Polling for Democracy: Public Opinion and Political Liberalization in Mexico* (1996). ISBN 0-8420-2583-9

Brian Loveman and Thomas M. Davies, Jr., eds., *The Politics of Antipolitics: The Military in Latin America*, 3d ed., revised and updated (1996). Cloth ISBN 0-8420-2609-6 Paper ISBN 0-8420-2611-8

Joseph S. Tulchin, Andrés Serbín, and Rafael Hernández, eds., *Cuba and the Caribbean: Regional Issues and Trends in the Post-Cold War Era* (1997). ISBN 0-8420-2652-5

Thomas W. Walker, ed., *Nicaragua without Illusions: Regime Transition and Structural Adjustment in the 1990s* (1997). Cloth ISBN 0-8420-2578-2 Paper ISBN 0-8420-2579-0

Dianne Walta Hart, *Undocumented in L.A.: An Immigrant's Story* (1997). Cloth ISBN 0-8420-2648-7 Paper ISBN 0-8420-2649-5

Jaime E. Rodríguez O. and Kathryn Vincent, eds., *Myths, Misdeeds, and Misunderstandings: The Roots of Conflict in U.S.-Mexican Relations* (1997). ISBN 0-8420-2662-2

Jaime E. Rodríguez O. and Kathryn Vincent, eds., *Common Border, Uncommon Paths: Race, Culture, and National Identity in U.S.-Mexican Relations* (1997). ISBN 0-8420-2673-8

William H. Beezley and Judith Ewell, eds., *The Human Tradition in Modern Latin America* (1997). Cloth ISBN 0-8420-2612-6   Paper ISBN 0-8420-2613-4

Donald F. Stevens, ed., *Based on a True Story: Latin American History at the Movies* (1997). Cloth ISBN 0-8420-2582-0 Paper ISBN 0-8420-2781-5

Jaime E. Rodríguez O., ed., *The Origins of Mexican National Politics, 1808–1847* (1997). Paper ISBN 0-8420-2723-8

Che Guevara, *Guerrilla Warfare*, with revised and updated introduction and case studies by Brian Loveman and Thomas M. Davies, Jr., 3d ed. (1997). Cloth ISBN 0-8420-2677-0   Paper ISBN 0-8420-2678-9

Adrian A. Bantjes, *As If Jesus Walked on Earth: Cardenismo, Sonora, and the Mexican Revolution* (1998; rev. ed., 2000). Cloth ISBN 0-8420-2653-3 Paper ISBN 0-8420-2751-3

Henry A. Dietz and Gil Shidlo, eds., *Urban Elections in Democratic Latin America* (1998). Cloth ISBN 0-8420-2627-4 Paper ISBN 0-8420-2628-2

A. Kim Clark, *The Redemptive Work: Railway and Nation in Ecuador, 1895–1930* (1998). Cloth ISBN 0-8420-2674-6 Paper ISBN 0-8420-5013-2

Joseph S. Tulchin, ed., with Allison M. Garland, *Argentina: The Challenges of Modernization* (1998). ISBN 0-8420-2721-1

Louis A. Pérez, Jr., ed., *Impressions of Cuba in the Nineteenth Century: The Travel Diary of Joseph J. Dimock* (1998). Cloth ISBN 0-8420-2657-6 Paper ISBN 0-8420-2658-4

June E. Hahner, ed., *Women through Women's Eyes: Latin American Women in Nineteenth-Century Travel Accounts* (1998). Cloth ISBN 0-8420-2633-9 Paper ISBN 0-8420-2634-7

James P. Brennan, ed., *Peronism and Argentina* (1998). ISBN 0-8420-2706-8

John Mason Hart, ed., *Border Crossings: Mexican and Mexican-American Workers*

(1998). Cloth ISBN 0-8420-2716-5
Paper ISBN 0-8420-2717-3

Brian Loveman, *For* la Patria: *Politics and the Armed Forces in Latin America* (1999). Cloth ISBN 0-8420-2772-6
Paper ISBN 0-8420-2773-4

Guy P. C. Thomson, with David G. LaFrance, *Patriotism, Politics, and Popular Liberalism in Nineteenth-Century Mexico: Juan Francisco Lucas and the Puebla Sierra* (1999).
ISBN 0-8420-2683-5

Robert Woodmansee Herr, in collaboration with Richard Herr, *An American Family in the Mexican Revolution* (1999).
ISBN 0-8420-2724-6

Juan Pedro Viqueira Albán, trans. Sonya Lipsett-Rivera and Sergio Rivera Ayala, *Propriety and Permissiveness in Bourbon Mexico* (1999).
Cloth ISBN 0-8420-2466-2
Paper ISBN 0-8420-2467-0

Stephen R. Niblo, *Mexico in the 1940s: Modernity, Politics, and Corruption* (1999).
Cloth ISBN 0-8420-2794-7
Paper (2001) ISBN 0-8420-2795-5

David E. Lorey, *The U.S.-Mexican Border in the Twentieth Century* (1999).
Cloth ISBN 0-8420-2755-6
Paper ISBN 0-8420-2756-4

Joanne Hershfield and David R. Maciel, eds., *Mexico's Cinema: A Century of Films and Filmmakers* (2000). Cloth ISBN 0-8420-2681-9 Paper ISBN 0-8420-2682-7

Peter V. N. Henderson, *In the Absence of Don Porfirio: Francisco León de la Barra and the Mexican Revolution* (2000).
ISBN 0-8420-2774-2

Mark T. Gilderhus, *The Second Century: U.S.-Latin American Relations since 1889* (2000). Cloth ISBN 0-8420-2413-1
Paper ISBN 0-8420-2414-X

Catherine Moses, *Real Life in Castro's Cuba* (2000). Cloth ISBN 0-8420-2836-6
Paper ISBN 0-8420-2837-4

K. Lynn Stoner, ed./comp., with Luis Hipólito Serrano Pérez, *Cuban and Cuban-American Women: An Annotated Bibliography* (2000).
ISBN 0-8420-2643-6

Thomas D. Schoonover, *The French in Central America: Culture and Commerce, 1820–1930* (2000).
ISBN 0-8420-2792-0

Enrique C. Ochoa, *Feeding Mexico: The Political Uses of Food since 1910* (2000). ISBN 0-8420-2812-9

Thomas W. Walker and Ariel C. Armony, eds., *Repression, Resistance, and Democratic Transition in Central America* (2000). Cloth ISBN 0-8420-2766-1   Paper ISBN 0-8420-2768-8

William H. Beezley and David E. Lorey, eds., *¡Viva México! ¡Viva la Independencia! Celebrations of September 16* (2001).
Cloth ISBN 0-8420-2914-1
Paper ISBN 0-8420-2915-X

Jeffrey M. Pilcher, *Cantinflas and the Chaos of Mexican Modernity* (2001).
Cloth ISBN 0-8420-2769-6
Paper ISBN 0-8420-2771-8

Victor M. Uribe-Uran, ed., *State and Society in Spanish America during the Age of Revolution* (2001). Cloth ISBN 0-8420-2873-0   Paper ISBN 0-8420-2874-9

Andrew Grant Wood, *Revolution in the Street: Women, Workers, and Urban Protest in Veracruz, 1870–1927* (2001).
ISBN 0-8420-2879-X

Charles Bergquist, Ricardo Peñaranda, and Gonzalo Sánchez G., eds., *Violence in Colombia, 1990–2000: Waging War and Negotiating Peace* (2001).
Cloth ISBN 0-8420-2869-2
Paper ISBN 0-8420-2870-6

William Schell, Jr., *Integral Outsiders: The American Colony in Mexico City, 1876–1911* (2001). ISBN 0-8420-2838-2

John Lynch, *Argentine Caudillo: Juan Manuel de Rosas* (2001).
Cloth ISBN 0-8420-2897-8
Paper ISBN 0-8420-2898-6

Samuel Basch, M.D., ed. and trans. Fred D. Ullman, *Recollections of Mexico: The Last Ten Months of Maximilian's Empire* (2001). ISBN 0-8420-2962-1

David Sowell, *The Tale of Healer Miguel Perdomo Neira: Medicine, Ideologies, and Power in the Nineteenth-Century Andes* (2001).
Cloth ISBN 0-8420-2826-9
Paper ISBN 0-8420-2827-7

June E. Hahner, ed., *A Parisian in Brazil: The Travel Account of a Frenchwoman in Nineteenth-Century Rio de Janeiro* (2001). Cloth ISBN 0-8420-2854-4
Paper ISBN 0-8420-2855-2

Richard A. Warren, *Vagrants and Citizens: Politics and the Masses in Mexico City from Colony to Republic* (2001).
ISBN 0-8420-2964-8

Roderick J. Barman, *Princess Isabel of Brazil: Gender and Power in the Nineteenth Century* (2002).
Cloth ISBN 0-8420-2845-5
Paper ISBN 0-8420-2846-3